W9-AWO-292

Praise for
Shake Up Learning

"Kasey Bell has been shaking up my learning since she started blogging in 2014. She has a fresh, exciting perspective that helps educators innovate and improve in an approachable, friendly way. No geek speak here—just fresh ideas, a can-do attitude, and a love for children. That is what we all need to shake up learning, and this is the book and educator to help you do just that! Kasey is an awesome person and an incredible educator, and this book is a remarkable contribution to education."

—Vicki Davis, @coolcatteacher, host of *The 10-Minute Teacher* podcast

▶ ▶ ▶

"This is *the* book for educators wanting to transform their classrooms and schools into dynamic hubs of learning and curiosity. I was hooked from page one, and it was so captivating that I could not put the book down! Kasey creates a compelling mix of both personal and inspirational stories to motivate and inspire every educator. She makes it easy to see how we can use technology to create dynamic learning experiences for our kids that break the mold and allow us to enter into a new frontier of learning. This book offers a great synergy of the why and *how* and has something in it for every teacher. Don't miss your chance to learn from one of the best in this educational page-turner!"

—Holly Clark, coauthor of *The Google Infused Classroom*

▶ ▶ ▶

"Kasey is one of my favorite educators to learn from, and this book is essential for all levels of educators. Kasey's honest approach helps bridge the gap between the big ideas in education and the practical strategies that help teachers create dynamic learning experiences for every student. This is not a book about technology. This is a book about *learning*!"

—Alice Keeler, coauthor of *50 Things You Can Do with Google Classroom*

▶ ▶ ▶

"Kasey Bell's charming personality bursts out of the pages of this book. Her fresh perspective on revolutionizing the classroom gives teachers the reasons to push boundaries and take learning to new heights. Her practical ideas empower teachers with innovative ways to truly shake things up!"

—Tony Vincent, learning and technology educator, Tony Vincent, Inc., learninginhand.com

"Whether you are a longtime fan of Kasey Bell or just interested in shaking up learning, this book will not disappoint. Each chapter thoughtfully includes discussion and reflection questions as well as chapter actions. Baked into the Dynamic Learning Experience casserole that is this book are witty pop cultural references and frank and honest approaches to integrating technology, the 4 Cs, learning, and leading. Kasey's personality, voice, and years of experience are baked into every chapter with personal and candid stories of success, failure, and teachable moments. If you are looking to move beyond your grade level and subject, beyond the tools, beyond the due date, beyond the bell, or beyond the walls of your classroom, Kasey provides an easy recipe with a variety of ingredients and methods to meet you where you are and help you reach your vision."

—**Lisa Johnson, CEO and founder, Techchef4u and author**
of *Cultivating Communication in the Classroom*

"Kasey Bell puts her finger on the pulse of education in *Shake Up Learning*. The dynamic learning framework she outlines in the book describes the kind of meaningful, authentic learning that students are craving. With discussion questions, a companion website, and room to reflect, this book is packed with resources!"

—**Matt Miller, speaker, blogger, and author of *Ditch That Textbook***

"Kasey's book makes you feel like you're having a conversation with a friend—a very persuasive, very knowledgeable friend—who just happens to know exactly what you need to hear to change education where and when it counts: in your own classroom, tomorrow.

"This book has a homegrown style that is going to speak to the practical nature of teachers everywhere. Forget lofty idealism that has left you wondering, *Okay, but what do I actually do tomorrow in my classroom?* This book answers that question. There's a *why*, but more importantly, there's a *what* that, as we've all come to expect from Kasey, is clear, well-organized, approachable, and is going to make each reader feel ready to begin the process of shaking up learning in his or her classroom."

—**Amy Mayer, CEO, friEdTechnology**

"Educational books that engage both the heart and the mind are rare, but an educational technology book that can teach WHY we should be trying things in addition to HOW are even rarer. Kasey Bell does both with *Shake Up Learning*. She gives detailed steps to help any educator at any level of technology expertise, embrace a growth mindset and be willing to make changes—changes needed to education in a way that doesn't threaten or intimidate, but instead allow you to see the other side of integration in a comprehensive and *fun* manner. As an administrator, I appreciate the energy and direction Kasey provides while giving examples and options for educators. This book is grounded in purpose . . . and is a resource that will let both teachers and students thrive."

—**Amber Teamann, principal, Wylie ISD and coauthor of** *Education Write Now*

"With a heart and passion as big as her smile and as warm as her Texan 'y'all,' Kasey fills our minds and our hearts as she reminds us of the power we have to push our learning and stretch our teaching. Her dynamic approach encourages us to step out of our comfort zone, change our teaching practices, and be driven to prepare our students for an ever-changing, technology-driven world. Most of all, Kasey's honest and to-the-heart words connect her ideas, writing, and resources to all educators' experiences and empower all of us to be the very best we can be for each student every day."

—**Carrie Baughcum, special education teacher and creator of CarrieBaughcum.com**

"As I read through Kasey's work, I find my mind dancing between visions of student learning, my own productivity, and the larger global impact of being a tech-forward, connected educator. Through thought-provoking questions, real-world applications, and even space to wonder and dream, *Shake Up Learning* is more of an experience than a book. I can't wait to see how classrooms all over the globe will grow and evolve because of Kasey's touch!"

—**Cate Tolnai, director of member engagement, CUE**

shake Up Learning

Practical Ideas to Move **LEARNING** from Static to **DYNAMIC**

KASEY BELL

Shake Up Learning

© 2018 by Kasey Bell

All rights reserved. No part of this publication may be reproduced in any form or by any electronic or mechanical means, including information storage and retrieval systems, without permission in writing by the publisher, except by a reviewer who may quote brief passages in a review. For information regarding permission, contact the publisher at books@daveburgessconsulting.com.

This book is available at special discounts when purchased in quantity for use as premiums, promotions, fundraisers, or for educational use. For inquiries and details, contact the publisher at books@daveburgessconsulting.com.

Published by Dave Burgess Consulting, Inc.
San Diego, CA
http://daveburgessconsulting.com

Cover Design by Genesis Kohler
Editing and Interior Design by My Writers' Connection

ISTE Standards for Students, ©2016, ISTE (International Society for Technology in Education), iste.org. All rights reserved.

Library of Congress Control Number: 2018936386
Paperback ISBN: 978-1-946444-69-1
Ebook ISBN: 978-1-946444-70-7

First Printing: March 2018

Dedication

To my parents, Glenn and Marilyn Bell,
thank you for all your love, support, and encouragement.

To Mom, thank you for giving me a love of writing,
literature, and all things creative and bold.

To Dad, thank you for giving me a love of science and
technology, and all things "gadgety" and cool.

Contents

The Companion Website and Your Free Gift

As a way of saying thanks for your purchase, I'm offering a free download that's exclusive to readers of *Shake Up Learning*.

Your FREE Quick-Start Guide

With the *Shake Up Learning* Quick-Start Guide, you'll discover a printable reference guide of the main ideas, strategies, and tips from the book. Everything you need to get started with Dynamic Learning Experiences is included in the PDF that's part of the free companion website, ShakeUpLearningBook.com.

The Companion Website

I've created a companion website that includes many resources mentioned throughout this book.

Here are just a few things I've included:

- The *Shake Up Learning* Quick-Start Guide, which is a printable reference guide of the main ideas, strategies, and tips from the book
- A dedicated webpage for each chapter of the book, including clickable resources
- The Dynamic Learning Experience (DLE) searchable database of lessons from teachers like you where you can find ideas AND share your own
- Information about the companion course, The Dynamic Learning Workshop, which is a self-paced online course to enrich your learning with the book even more
- Special bonus materials and downloads

I will be adding more goodies to this website in the months to come. So if you're interested in expanding on what you've learned in this book, check out the following link:

ShakeUpLearningBook.com

Join the Community

Fans and readers of *Shake Up Learning* make up an extraordinary community of like-minded educators who are dedicated to making a difference in the lives of students. They wake up each day ready to shake up learning! As creator of *Shake Up Learning*, it was my responsibility to create an online space where readers and fans could go to connect, get encouragement, share ideas, support one another, and discuss *Shake Up Learning* blog posts, resources, and this book.

Just go to **shakeup.link/community** to join the Shake Up Learning community of inspired educators. Here you can connect with others who are also practicing the ideas shared in this book and find additional support on your journey.

I'll be moderating the community and checking in regularly. I look forward to seeing you there!

If you'd like to connect with me on Twitter or Instagram, follow @ShakeUpLearning.

The Companion Course: The Dynamic Learning Workshop

In addition to the community and website of free resources to support you, I am also offering an online course: The Dynamic Learning Workshop. This is a workshop designed to go deeper than just a book study and to not only explore the ideas in the book but bring them to life through video-based learning and support.

To find out more about the Dynamic Learning Workshop and how to enroll, go to **shakeup.link/DLworkshop**.

- Bulk pricing is available for large groups, campuses, or entire school districts.
- Purchase Orders are accepted.

Hey, y'all! Bless your heart for picking up this book written by a crazy Texas teacher! I was born bold, opinionated, a little bit geeky, and with an East Texas drawl dripping off my tongue. It is no coincidence that I have an affinity for technology, learning, and entrepreneurship. I grew up around technology in a family of entrepreneurs. My family owned and operated a drive-in theater from the late 1940s to the early 1980s in Paris, Texas, my hometown. My grandmother later became the primary owner of the 271 Drive-In Theater in Paris, Texas, during a time when it was rare to find female-owned businesses. The drive-in was passed on to my parents, who operated the theater on the weekends along with a full-time electronics business, Bell Electronics. During that time, my parents worked seven days a week. To say I had a good example of hard work, ingenuity, service, and grit would be an understatement. I always had strong role models in my life and on every side, and industrious women who never let their gender hold them back. My accent may have faded, but my roots run deep!

I grew up around movie projectors, juke boxes, satellite dishes, televisions, stereos, microphones, and the smell of fresh popcorn. My parents were the first on the block to have a microwave, and later the first to have a home computer. I was very blessed. When I received my first home stereo, computer, or any other piece of technology, my dad wouldn't put it together for me. He would hand me the box and say, "You do it." He wanted me to figure it out because he knew that was how I would learn. I was never afraid to tinker. It was encouraged in my house. I'm a nerd by nature and nurture! I'm a two-time Space Camper blessed by the good Lord and by God-fearing parents.

I found my calling as a teacher. My teaching career began as a middle school language arts teacher. I enjoyed language arts and literature, but I was never really passionate about the content. I was passionate about helping kids. I always loved finding ways to integrate technology in my classroom, take risks, and try new things that other teachers wouldn't. It wasn't long before other teachers would come to me for help with technology, asking, "How'd you do that?"

After discovering my passion for instructional technology and digital learning, I pursued a master's degree in educational technology. I had found my niche. These were my people! I loved every minute of it, and I became passionate about finding ways to help more teachers and impact more students.

I am still a teacher, though no longer teaching in a traditional K–12 classroom. Judge me if you will, but I teach teachers and would argue they are sometimes more challenging than my middle school students ever were. I believe teaching is a calling, and I am a teacher twenty-four hours a day, seven days a week. Every move I make can be judged and often is: every post, every idea, every question. Mistakes are often inflated. Questions are never ending. But I love it!

Our personal passions might vary greatly, but if you are reading this book, I suspect we share a passion for learning and doing what's best for kids. I want to stimulate student learning and prepare students to be successful in an ever-changing and technology-driven world. Our educational system is in desperate need of a shake up! It is antiquated and in need of a paradigm shift that will take our kids off the conveyor belt and guide them down personalized learning paths where they will learn new skills and gain new perspectives. Shaking things up—this is my jam. It's what I do. We don't have to keep doing things the way they have always been done. Technology is not a solution, but an opportunity to improve learning. Traditional learning doesn't cut it anymore. We must think differently about learning and not be afraid to be a little disruptive, to buck tradition thinking. I want to help teachers shake up learning, do things differently, and make a difference in the world of education.

Teachers and students live in a culture of testing and prescribed curriculums that do not always fit the needs of our students or the needs of the future workforce. If we shake up learning in our classes, in our schools, and in our districts, we could increase engagement and create a generation of skilled and innovative citizens. Y'all with me?

The Shake Up Learning Story

Before I committed to creating a blog, I was riddled with insecurities. I didn't think my voice mattered. Why would anyone listen to me when so many other educators were sharing incredible resources online and doing it better than I ever could? What could I share that was new and original? Content creation was for the chosen few, the education rock stars. Why would I want to leave my perfectly comfortable position as a lurker on the sidelines? What if I was a complete failure? What if I put something out there and no one read it? Worse, what if they read it and laughed at me?

I had started a blog several times with the best of intentions, spending countless hours researching platforms, templates, plugins, hosting options, and titles, but I never got my feet off the ground. Nothing was ever good enough. I was a perfectionist with paralysis. Many of us struggle with this fear. It's scary to put yourself out there!

I knew the value of blogging. When I was a classroom teacher, my students blogged, and they discovered the power of sharing their voices online and connecting with their peers. I saw an immediate change in the quality of their work. As an instructional leader and digital learning coach, I encouraged teachers to blog with their students. I was happy to help them get started and give them examples of teachers who do it well. However, I was not an example for them to follow.

When I finally resolved to take the plunge and start blogging, I wanted to launch my site not only with the perfect content but with the perfect design and logo that would stand out as perfection in the ever-crowded sea of educational bloggers. I wanted my blog to look like a well-established website before I ever let anyone see it. It simply had to be epic from day one. Right.

Eventually I got a grip and realized my blog would never be perfect. I let that dream go and focused on risk-taking, a skill on which I speak almost daily. I firmly believe in the power of taking risks, and I knew I could no longer allow my fears to hold me back. I also knew I could reach more teachers and students if I took the leap. So in January 2014, I put myself out there—I put my blog out there, imperfections and all!

The creation of *Shake Up Learning* was very intentional. When I decided to create a blog, I knew I didn't want it to be about me. No Kasey Bell dot com. Don't get me wrong, there's nothing wrong with using your name as the title of your blog, and I do actually own KaseyBell.com, just in case I ever need it. But I wanted everything about my educational blog to reflect my goal of affecting change and helping more teachers embrace digital tools as a means to transform the classroom. After a great deal of thought and research, *Shake Up Learning* was born.

When I published for the first time, I was terrified. I really don't know why. It's not like I was going to show up first—or even third or fourth—in a Google search, but I was scared of what people would think. I had seen the horrible trolls and commenters that were rampant on blogs, and I was worried about how critical other educators might be. It turns out my readers and other educational bloggers are very forgiving and supportive. I had no idea the wealth of support that was waiting for me.

I made some mistakes, but I survived. I was mortified the first time someone pointed to an error on my blog, and I'm talking about just a typo, nothing huge. Though the criticism was constructive and friendly, I took it personally and worried about it for days. But I kept going, and the more content I created, the more support I felt from readers, and the more my insecurities melted away. My skin grew a little thicker, and the affirmation and appreciation I received far outweighed the critical voices in my head. Learning from my mistakes was vital. I can't emphasize this enough. I find I always learn so much more from the moments that didn't go as planned. As tough as they can be to swallow, our mistakes shape our life's path. <u>Some of the best lessons I learned</u>—in academia and in life—<u>came from a misstep, taking a wrong turn, and sometimes falling flat on my face. I still make a lot of mistakes, but I have learned to let them go.</u>

Another surprising skill I have learned along the way is to accept criticism and consider it an opportunity to improve, not a validation of my worst fears. If people only ever see your best self, they never see the real you. Just listen to the bloopers from my podcast,

GoogleTeacherTribe.com, and you'll know what I mean. Most of the time, criticism from my fellow educators is offered with kindness. I am lucky to be in a community of educators governed by grace and overwhelming support for one another. It's not always like that in other professions.

Back in 2014, I never expected blogging to flip my career on its head, but that's exactly what happened. I had no clue about the transformation—the shake up, if you will—that was about to take place. The truth is, I never thought about the community I was joining as a blogger or the community I was creating until it was there in front of me. Teachers began leaving comments on my blog, sharing their ideas and significantly expanding my personal learning network. The comments and conversations were, for the most part, warm and positive. My blog has connected with some of the most inspiring teachers in the world. And to think, I almost let my fears keep me from such wonderful opportunities to learn and grow. Stepping outside my comfort zone was the best decision I ever made.

About This Book

As I continued to grow my blog and its readership, I watched as many fellow bloggers took the next step and published a book. My first thought was, *That will never be me.* Followed up by *What would I write about?* and *I'm not good enough to put together an entire book!* Sound familiar? The same fears that kept me from blogging were telling me I couldn't write a book. Then I met Dave Burgess.

At the 2015 Revolutionizing Learning Conference in Royse City, Texas, I saw Dave Burgess dazzle the audience with the most dynamic keynote speech I had ever heard. I sat in the front row, eager to participate and learn from the Pirate himself.

Later I was in the library where Dave was signing his books and selling other books from his publishing company. As I browsed the collection, seeing the work of my colleagues and a couple I would even call friends, Dave walked over and asked, "When will we see your book on this table?" I was floored. First, Dave Burgess knew who I was, y'all. *Seriously?* Second, he thought I had the potential to be one of his published authors! Looking back, I can't even remember how I responded. I know I tried to play it cool, but inside I was scared, excited, and had suddenly started to believe I could do it. That's really all it took: I had to believe I could do it and that people would care enough to read what I would have to say—even if those people turned out to be Dave Burgess and my mom and dad.

So here we are! I have written a book—a book designed to inform you, inspire you, and help you transform the learning in your classroom in new ways. My book is intended to bridge the gap between the big ideas that inspire you and move you and the practical implementation of those ideas. My goal is to help classroom teachers make meaningful change. I want this book to spur you into action and inspire you to transform, not just sit on your bookshelf.

There are so many books available these days to help teachers understand a multitude of concepts. I am a prolific reader of education books, especially those that deal with technology. Many of these books are filled with pie-in-the-sky scenarios from educators with great ideas but no real follow-through, no real plan for bringing those ideas to fruition. Without that piece, a book is just sit-and-get professional learning. Action is the hard part, the part I usually refer to as "eating your veggies." Action is not only doing and learning, it's stepping out of your comfort zone and changing up your teaching practices. That kind of change can be uncomfortable and isn't always fun, but just as eating your veggies is good for your physical health, shaking up learning is amazing for your classroom health.

If you were hoping to read this book at the beach, be done in a couple hours, and never open it again, please reconsider. I believe the best use of this book is to read it—ideally, with some of your colleagues and peers—and then spend time pondering, debating, dreaming, journaling, and planning. This book can be as interactive as you want it to be, but it is up to you. I challenge you to push yourself to take action, share your journey with others, and take your learning to the next level. Oh, and if you are a perfect teacher, get out of here. This book is only for authentic teachers who are far from perfect.

How to Interact with This Book

I've created a companion website to make this experience more interactive for you as the reader. If you follow *Shake Up Learning*, you know that I love resources, and I have put together a website that is loaded with additional resources, including any new goodies I discover after the publishing of this book. Consider this your *Shake Up Learning* toolkit with dedicated pages for each chapter, plus resources, downloads, and a searchable lesson plan database for YOU! Don't miss out on this FREE resource or the FREE Quick-Start Guide, all available at **ShakeUpLearningBook.com**.

Each chapter contains questions to ponder on your own or discuss with your colleagues, as well as activities you can complete. My accompanying website, ShakeUpLearningBook.com, also offers supplemental materials and opportunities to connect, learn, and share all the ways you are shaking up learning. At the end of each chapter you will find the following:

- **Link to Chapter Resources**—Each chapter has a dedicated page on ShakeUpLearningBook.com where you can find resources mentioned in the chapter, as well as supplemental resources to help you extend the learning.

- **Discussion and Reflection Questions**—These questions are designed to help you think critically about the chapter and how it applies to you. You may use these as reflection questions to answer independently or discuss with your colleagues or book study group. You can also take it a step further and share your answers online in the Shake Up Learning Community (shakeup.link/community), or use the hashtag #ShakeUpLearning.

- **Chapter Actions**—Each chapter will also include some actions you can take, big or small, to use the material to affect changes in your role as a teacher. Choose one or choose them all; you are in charge!

- **Reflection Space**—I've included some blank real estate in this book to give you room to write, sketch, draw, doodle, whatever you need. I encourage you to take advantage of this process to help digest the book and the process and to reflect on any actions you have taken.

Here's a quick outline of what you'll find in the pages ahead:

Part 1: The Why: It's Time to Shake Up Learning

Rapidly evolving technology and the demands of the digital age are transforming not only the way we live but also the way we learn. One thing is for certain—educators cannot continue the status quo if they expect to equip young people for the world to come. The tools students are using are newer, sleeker, and faster than ever before. In some cases, the medium is even changing the message. Our advanced technology is changing our content—sometimes for better, sometimes for worse. In this section, we will explore why it is time to shake up learning, the historical changes that mirror the advancements and reactions in the twenty-first century. We will dig deeper into the way the Internet age has reshaped learning. We'll discover shifts in the job market and predictions for our students' futures, including the growth of entrepreneurship. As educators, we have a chance to use these changes to shake up learning.

Part 2: The What: The DNA of Dynamic Learning

Technological advancements present us with a unique opportunity to rethink education and the types of learning experiences we design for our students. This is an opportunity for learning that is more dynamic. Together, we will explore the groundwork for moving learning from static to dynamic. We'll analyze risk-taking, asking better questions, and breaking down bad habits that contribute to the game of school. We will also take a closer look at the value of connecting, sharing, and a continuous learning mindset, then journey on into the curation of resources and the power of sharing your story. Understanding the DNA makeup of Dynamic Learning will prepare us to take actions that will transform our old ways and preconceived notions.

Part 3: The How: Equipping for Impact

This book is all about action, and this section will focus on planning for action, how to implement the ideas in your classroom, and tips for success. We will learn how to plan meaningful Dynamic Learning Experiences and how to facilitate with finesse. We will also learn the importance of reflection and sharing. This is your chance to make meaningful change a reality!

THE WHY: IT'S TIME TO SHAKE UP LEARNING

As much as you love or hate change, it's inevitable, and it's affecting our schools and our number one priority: student learning. To be a change agent, you must grasp change both historically and with vision for the future. It's important that we as educators of the future workforce understand what twenty-first-century change means and how it has changed learning.

We are at a tipping point in education and on the verge of the paradigm shift that has been discussed for many years now. However, the barriers to the revolution have us stuck in the old ways. Not to say we haven't made progress, but we still have a long way to go.

A lot of people have been throwing technology at the problems in education, hoping for a panacea that will magically deliver us to the twenty-first century, but technology is not the answer. The shift that needs to happen in education starts with you and your drive to shake up learning.

Chapter 1
21st Century Change

The only thing constant is change.
—Heraclitus

Change is everywhere. Whether it's your status, your profile picture, your device, or following the latest trends, it's hip to change it up. Change—in all its forms—is not only trendy, it's *trending*. Change is so cool; it's the new black. In fact, by the time you finish this book, all kinds of changes will have occurred. A slew of new platforms and applications will have emerged. I hope your decision to read this book is a sign you are ready and willing to embrace change. Maybe you even embraced the digital version of this book. Maybe you're taking notes on a tablet. Maybe not. Either way, the future is here, and technology cannot be ignored. The exponential changes are staggering. It truly is a new frontier. New technologies are giving rise to new settlements—and new jobs, services, rules, and regulations—across the world's vast digital landscape, a digital Wild West.

Keeping up with the changes in education technology is one of the greatest challenges educators face. The pace at which digital tools are emerging is quite staggering. As an instructional technology specialist, digital learning coach, or whatever my newest title happens to be, my job is to help teachers understand how to use these tools in their classrooms to benefit students. The challenge is not only keeping up with new technologies released daily but also staying current on well-established applications such as G Suite, which are continually updated. It's a race we are not winning, nor will we ever. All we can do is try to filter out what is unnecessary and drill down to what is most worthwhile to give students and teachers the biggest bang for the buck.

A major drawback to this new reality of constant change is that most people don't like change. Think about it: What's the usual reaction among teachers when a new program or initiative is implemented on your campus? Change is stressful. Even young children resist change. Have you seen the YouTube videos of those adorable toddlers seeing their clean-shaven daddies for the first time? If you haven't, go to YouTube right now and search "Daddy shaved." I'll wait! Most of the children cry, some are scared, and a few even run and hide. Our negative reaction to change seems almost innate. It's confusing, frightening, and much of the time, we reject it.

Greek philosopher Heraclitus is known for saying, "The only thing constant is change." His words, first spoken around five hundred BC, still hold true. No matter what we do, the world will be a drastically different place in just a few years. We cannot predict the future, but we know there are changes that lie ahead. That's the one thing we know for sure.

Looking Back to Move Forward

Change has always been inevitable. Throughout time, our civilization has experienced historical periods of change and growth. We study the past because doing so empowers us to prepare for our future—and for the future that awaits our students. So let's travel back in time a bit and take a look at some historical changes and the impact on our world.

In the late nineteenth century, the world was changing rapidly. The Industrial Revolution redefined the way the world worked, including the design of the factory model of education we have today. It marked a major turning point in history, influencing almost every aspect of daily life, and a major turning point for education. Consider how this mirrors the changes we are seeing and the conversations we are hearing today.

By the early twentieth century, electricity and electric light were bringing even greater changes. Both innovations, particularly electric light, made modern life much easier. It seems so simple today, something we all take for granted. The invention of the practical incandescent light bulb resulted in lighting becoming one of the first publicly available applications of electrical power. It's difficult to imagine the world without electricity, let alone without electric light.

With new technology comes new fears. Although not without its own dangers, electricity replaced the naked flames of gas lighting and greatly reduced fire hazards within homes and factories. The sign in FIGURE 1.1 is one that actually appeared in a room that had been newly equipped with Edison Electric Light. Do you see what it says at the bottom? "The use of Electricity for lighting is in no way harmful to health, nor does it affect the soundness of sleep." Such concerns sound ludicrous today, but do we have similar fears of new technologies today, more than one hundred years later?

FIGURE 1.1

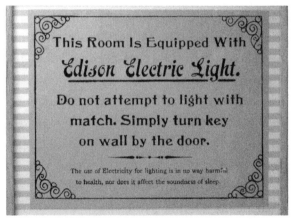

Wichary, Marcin, "This room is equipped with Edison Electric Light," Flickr, Sept. 2, 2006, www.flickr.com/photos/mwichary/2276499672/.

The Factory Model of Education

In Seth Godin's TEDx Youth Talk and eBook, *Stop Stealing Dreams (What Is School For?)*, he issues an imperative about a significant emergency in education today that is both economic and cultural. We are products of the Industrial Age. We should be asking the question, *What is school for?* School used to be for teaching obedience to produce factory workers. Public education was partially the result of getting cheap-labor children out of factory jobs so adults could step in. It was to prepare the next generation of compliant workers. This hand-me-down system, the factory school, must change.

Let's fast forward to the late twentieth and early twenty-first century. With the invention of space travel, computers, cell phones, the Internet, and countless other jaw-dropping innovations, today's world is changing faster than ever before. When you were young, what did you imagine about life in the twenty-first century? Is it as you predicted? Maybe we can take a play out of *Back to the Future* and compare our world to the future created in *Back to the Future 2*, which had Marty and Doc Brown traveling to the year 2015. Those screenwriters did a great job designing a futuristic world to tickle our imaginations! In that future, we saw flying cars, hover boards, newspapers that could magically change headlines right before your eyes, a watch that could tell you down to the second when the rain would stop, and of course, Marty's super-cool, self-lacing Nikes.

We laugh about it, but those *Back to the Future* writers were on to something. Think about it: Today you can actually get your hands on those Nikes on eBay. My Apple Watch has an app that tells me when it's about to start raining and how long the rain will last. And most news is digital these days, coming to us in real time and virtually rendering print newspapers a dying medium. I remember watching those films back in the day and dreaming of a futuristic world where I could fly around in a DeLorean. I'm not too sure how I feel about the DeLorean anymore, but the predictions were not far off.

So here we are in the twenty-first century. Welcome. We have been here for eighteen years already, and it's time to change the conversation. We have entered a time of unprecedented change that has left the Industrial Revolution in the dust. The conversation must refocus education back onto what matters most: preparing young people to live and learn in an ever-changing, post-modern world.

Historically, the educational system in the United States has been slow to change. Some of that stagnation has had to do with funding, bureaucracy, and politics, but some of the resistance is simply inherent. Education in America is largely based on the old factory model that was developed more than one hundred years ago. At that time, it served an important purpose and met many urgent needs, but it's a one-size-

It's 2018, and we are still using an educational model from the nineteenth and twentieth centuries!

fits-all model. Life has changed drastically since those days, and that model is no longer effective. The system is broken in so many ways, and just about any teacher, student, or parent would probably agree. It's 2018, and we are still using an educational model from the nineteenth and twentieth centuries! Something has to change, and I believe educators must lead the way. Teachers and administrators must be willing to see past the strongholds and buck the system to do what's best for kids. Do we want our kids to receive a hand-me-down education?

Online Resources for Chapter 1

Here you will find resources mentioned in Chapter 1, supplemental resources, videos, as well as new and updated resources.

ShakeUpLearningBook.com/1

Discussion Questions

- Think about how you learn in the twenty-first century. How it is changing?
- How are you preparing students to learn, live, and work in an ever-changing society?
- Think about your career so far. We all watch the pendulum swing back and forth when it comes to pedagogy and best practices in instruction and assessment. No matter where you are in your career path, as a teacher, you have seen change. How do you react to changes in your job, your classroom, your teaching? How do you react to new advancements in technology?
- As a teacher, or whatever your role in education, do you ever feel like you are part of the "factory"? Why or why not?

Chapter 1 Actions

- Twenty-first century teaching and learning is about more than buzzwords, so start a conversation with a colleague, a member of your personal learning network, or your administrator about how to shake up learning. Are you doing what's best for kids? Is your school part of the conversation?
- Join the global conversation on Twitter! Let's discuss twenty-first-century change and embrace the digital learning revolution with the Shake Up Learning hashtag: #ShakeUpLearning.
- Watch *Seth Godin: The School System (shakeup.link/youtu1ee8)*, and reflect on the argument he presents.
- Brainstorm three things you would like to see changed in your educational system.

Reflection Space

_____

_____

_____

_____

_____

_____

_____

_____

_____

_____

_____

_____

_____

_____

_____

_____

Chapter 2

Technology Has Changed the Way We Learn

The world has changed—and continues changing—rapidly and radically when it comes to the ways in which we can learn, and what knowledge, skills, dispositions, and forms of literacy our children will need to flourish in their futures.
—Will Richardson

Nowhere is twenty-first-century change more apparent than in technology and communication. The Internet—and the advent of living more and more of one's life online—has transformed the very act of being social and interacting with other humans. By the way, everything is social, or it soon will be! Social media is quickly becoming part of everything. I believe we will soon stop differentiating between websites as social or not, because eventually they will all have a social aspect. To take advantage of this sea of change, educators must understand they can no longer ignore social media. It's how we communicate, and its platforms and tools are necessary to cultivate leadership, facilitate professional learning, engage parents, and define our school brands. Most importantly, social media platforms and tools are vital to enhancing student learning. Remember when we thought Facebook would never have an application in education or on the job? Today Facebook and many other platforms are being used to improve communication and collaboration across the globe.

With the evolution of technology, a new language has emerged. These words now appear in Merriam-Webster's Unabridged Dictionary: FOMO, clickbait, emoji, jegging, meme, Bitcoin, athleisure, hella, ICYMI, and nomophobia. If you don't know some of these words, Google them! Do you speak this new language? Are any of these words part of your everyday vocabulary? Would you say you are fluent?

It might seem silly now, but understanding the changes happening around us requires the acquisition of a new vocabulary. I'm not saying you have to run around screaming, "YOLO!" (You Only Live Once), but be willing to embrace the reality that our new world has a new language. I guarantee your students are speaking in this language, and as an educator, you are most effective when you communicate with them in ways they understand. It also gives you an opportunity to model positive and professional behavior for students to emulate.

With information being created and shared so quickly these days, educators must adapt, adjust, and be willing to learn new skills and vocabulary. A teacher's job is never done!

If we are to ever truly move beyond technology as a substitution, we must get rid of terms that are rooted in old school, paper-based assignments: paperless, notebook, packet, worksheet, poster, cards, portfolio, etc. Vocabulary can limit our perception of what's possible. An interactive notebook could simply be taking the paper-based notebook and images and putting them online in a presentation software. But again, that limits the possibilities. We need new, creative words. What if instead of *notebook*, a word that soon will have very little meaning for future-ready students, it becomes something new, like a "Learning Stream" or a "Learning Binge"?

With that in mind, let's look beyond 2018 and into the future. What's next? What kind of world are you preparing your students for? I'm sure you hear this idea often. Schools are expected to prepare students for jobs that don't exist yet, but no one knows exactly what the future holds. It is one big question mark.

Are you talking to your stuff yet? If not, you will be soon. Everything—from cell phones to crockpots—is getting smarter, more connected, and giving us more ways to automate our lives. The Internet of Things or IoT is just the beginning. The technology gets better, faster, and stronger every day. I have regular interactions with my Google Assistant, Alexa (from my Amazon Echo), and Siri on my iPhone. I mostly talk to my stuff when no one else is around because I'm not sure the world is ready, but it will be.

Think back to the early days of cell phones when only a few people had them. I was just a kid, but, as I mentioned, my parents were early adopters when it came to technology. I was always so embarrassed when they would call me and I had to use my cell phone in front of other people. Today, cell phones and wearable technology are everywhere. But I still hesitate to go all Dick Tracy with my Apple Watch in public.

We are just scratching the surface of what this technology can do. Machine learning and artificial intelligence are only going to improve. Every platform, every app that is worth its salt is now incorporating speech-to-text and text-to-speech capabilities. The need for keyboarding skills will drastically dissipate. Don't get me wrong—my ninth-grade keyboarding class taught me some valuable typing skills. I needed those to write this book in an efficient manner. But the next generation will not need those typing skills.

Your new life is loading right now—think about that for a moment. What lies ahead? We are still in the early years of the twenty-first century. What will the lives of our students look like in another couple of decades? Technology is changing lives in profound ways, and it is definitely changing the lives of our students.

Learning has changed, and it will continue to change. Before we can tackle all the technological changes in our classrooms, we must first take a step back and redefine what learning is and what it looks like in the twenty-first century. Technology has not only changed the way we learn—how we access and acquire new information and skills—but also the need for different types of learning. Teachers are no longer the gatekeepers of content. It is free and readily accessible from just about any device, around the clock. If you are hanging onto the idea of just giving students informational content, you and your students are going to be left behind. If you are afraid of new technology, expect to become obsolete.

Consider your own learning. What's a new skill you've acquired in the past five to eight years? How did you learn it? What was new or different about that experience? In a world of instant information, the value of rote memorization has sharply declined. Our textbooks are out of date by the time they reach the printer. Reading and memorizing dates and information might produce a passing grade on a standardized test, but it will not prepare students for the workforce of the future.

Companies are also changing the way they provide professional learning to their employees. Employees get to decide when, where, and how they will learn, teach, and collaborate with each other to innovate and grow the company. Educators must do the same. We must rethink the way we support the learning and growth of our K–12 students and how we'll improve our own professional learning.

Here's an interesting side note about how learning has changed: While technology has overhauled the job market and economy, it has also presented us with new ways to explore learning that don't require technology. Please don't misunderstand my point. Technology is not a necessary component for learning, obviously, but the influence of the changes to the job market and the way the world learns has presented us with

SHIFT YOUR MINDSET

The key to making any meaningful changes always starts with a solid foundation and that oh-so-trendy word, *mindset*. You'll find a lot of the concepts and ideas presented in this section require a shift in mindset. They require you to think differently, to let go of preconceived notions about teaching and learning. The mind is a powerful thing. Having a growth mindset means being open to a shift in traditional education and pushing the normal bounds of school, and it is necessary to truly shake up learning.

Mindset also poses the greatest roadblock when introducing technology into the classroom. I cannot count the times I hear, "I'm just not good with technology!" That is a limiting belief. Make up your mind to be positive. The classroom is already full of obstacles. Technology doesn't have to become a burden. Maybe you aren't as quick to learn with technology as your peers, but never let that become an excuse. If your mind is holding you back, you have some internal work to do. Take the time to reflect on your current mindset and prepare yourself to be open to the ideas and actions in this book.

new opportunities to expand our instructional strategies and to personalize learning in ways never conceived before. Technology has opened the door for new learning.

Do you remember what happened to the companies that ignored advancements in technology? Companies like Blockbuster, Kodak, and Radio Shack were almost blown off the map because they didn't grow and adapt. Let's make sure this doesn't happen to our students. Let's have more vision than Blockbuster. Our students deserve it.

At this point, I fervently hope you are not still hiding your head in the sand or thinking the digital revolution is just a fad. I can promise you that it isn't a fad. We are in the middle of a critical shift in education, and it's being met with resistance at every level. On which side of the fence are you? Are you afraid to jump into social media? Do you resist using new technology in the classroom? If so, I want to help you reverse course and lead the way by fearlessly letting go of the antiquated, industrial age model of traditional education and embracing some new ideas. Technology is undeniably improving many aspects of our lives. I want to make sure it's improving our students' learning experiences, and that's where you come in! Stretch your classroom flexibility. What do you think of when you think of someone who is flexible? Someone who is easily adapted to change.

Online Resources for Chapter 2

Here you will find resources mentioned in Chapter 2, supplemental resources, videos, as well as new and updated resources.

ShakeUpLearningBook.com/2

Discussion Questions

- How has technology changed your personal life? Professional life?
- In planning your next lesson, ask yourself, *Will these learning goals help prepare my students for the future?* If the answer is no, what modifications could you make?
- What actions can you take to learn the new vocabulary?
- If your new life is still loading, what do you think lies ahead?
- How has twenty-first-century change affected your classroom, your teaching style, and your mindset?
- What concepts and skills are still being taught that we need to discard?

Technology Has Changed the Way We Learn

Chapter 2 Actions

- Read "4 Ways Digital Tech Has Changed K–12 Learning" from *T.H.E. Journal* (shakeup.link/4ways1d61)
- Watch this video: "New Learning for a Rapidly Changing World" (shakeup.link/youtu68c6) and reflect on the ideas presented.
- Start a discussion about change with your class and find out what your students think.

Reflection Space

→ Chapter 3 ↠
The Rise of the Entrepreneur

*The industrial age is over. It's dead. The idea of going
to school to get a job is an obsolete idea! A steady paycheck
is an industrial age idea.*
—Robert Kiyosaki, author of *Rich Dad, Poor Dad*

Technology is not simply changing the way we learn and communicate; it's upending the way we earn a living. Look around. We are witnessing the rise of the entrepreneur. According to a 2010 study by Intuit, 40 percent of the US workforce will be self-employed. It has never been easier to become an entrepreneur, and this simple fact is changing the landscape of business. It should also be changing K–12 and higher education. With widespread access to the Internet, just about anyone—students, teachers, guidance counselors, principals—can get an online business up and running with relatively little start-up cost and almost no technical expertise. Many teachers are finding ways to share resources and bring in additional income, giving rise to the new moniker "teacherprenuer." Most importantly, the entrepreneurial learning environment is shifting the way the world learns.

The American dream is fading. It wasn't that long ago the American dream meant something very specific. Essentially, it meant working a steady job for eight hours a day, five days a week.

You'd have career security and work there for thirty-plus years. You'd live in an adequate house in a safe neighborhood with two cars and two kids, maybe even a dog. Those days are over. We no longer have guarantees of job security, and the original American dream continues to fade every year.

Currently we still live under the illusion that the workplace is a secure place to spend the rest of your life. For the first time in history, children might not do as well as their parents. Job security is declining. What worked for previous generations isn't working as well for people today.

In his book, *Tribes: We Need You to Lead Us*, Seth Godin claims stability is an illusion. "It's human nature—we still assume the world is stable, still assume that Google will be number one in five years, that we'll type on keyboards and fly on airplanes, that China will keep growing, and that the polar ice cap won't really be melted in six years. And we're wrong."

With a shifting economy and less job stability, people of all ages, but especially millennials, are defining a new breed of business owners. Author Daniel Pink calls this the "Free Agent Nation," individuals choosing to leave their organizations to go out on their own. On a global basis, everything is being turned upside down because of rapidly advancing technologies that are eliminating many jobs, and we are left with people who are not prepared for the jobs that remain.

The Internet start-up has contributed significantly to the changing landscape, and our students will live in a more participatory economy where they can create and define their own unique jobs and careers. It's time for schools to accept that simply preparing students to be a part of the compliant work force is not enough. I imagine it's not often that you hear a student say, "When I grow up, I want to work in a factory!"

Remember the sign that would hang at a business and tell customers how long it had been around? "Established in 1925." That used to be an advantage, conveying value and success and longevity. Today it could be more of a hindrance, signaling to customers the business might be old-school or antiquated in its approach. That's a real problem when most consumers are seeking the next big thing.

Whether you agree or not, this shift presents a huge opportunity for students to be remarkable. It's not just millennials and high-level corporate executives, either. More than a dozen teachers have become millionaires on Teachers Pay Teachers. Digital tools have opened a whole new marketplace for teachers to find, share, and create new digital materials for the classroom in this new economy.

Entrepreneurial organizations are centered on learning, which means most processes involve learning how to work. Taking ownership of the learning process is satisfying, as is the reward in creating a final product. Entrepreneurs have authority over their time, where they spend their energy and effort, what they create, the partners they choose, and input and feedback into every step of the process. None of that freedom is present in the factory model of education.

This consistent daily quest for knowledge is one of the most gratifying processes of entrepreneurial life. Due to the need for constant learning and self-improvement, entrepreneurs are constantly learning by creating and altering the structure of their organizations, and the

> This shift presents a huge opportunity for students to be remarkable.

power might shift depending on the current need of the business.

This trend toward entrepreneurship also requires new skills in order to be successful. Does our current curriculum support the entrepreneurial skill set? What do these entrepreneurial opportunities represent for our students? What does it mean for the learning environment? What skills do students need to survive in this changing economy?

To become successful entrepreneurs, students must be allowed to practice the art of curiosity. They must learn how to take risks and become resilient, as well as how to take ownership of their learning. Creative thinking and problem-solving are must-have skills for any twenty-first-century entrepreneur. Students need opportunities to approach problems in their own way and develop creative solutions. In an automated world, creative solutions will help businesses stand apart from the field. Machine learning and artificial intelligence will eventually take over many mundane tasks and the problems we need to solve in our day-to-day world. But these machines are far from being able to replicate the creativity and innovation of a young mind!

In his book *Deep Work*, Cal Newport argues there are two core abilities needed to thrive in this new economy—the ability to quickly master difficult things and the ability to produce at an elite level in terms of both quality and speed. Are we teaching students to master difficult tasks, to dig in, to build grit? What do students produce in your class? Are they learning how to quickly synthesize information? Do they create high-quality content, whether that's a blog post, a report, a hypothesis, or a performance? How can we give students more opportunities to produce at an elite level?

With learning at our fingertips, traditional schooling and learning methods are being pushed to the wayside. A college degree doesn't mean what it once did. Let me be clear—I worked hard for all my degrees and experienced deep learning and challenges that brought me to where I am today. But the idea of attending a school or college or university primarily to obtain a specific job is an industrial-age idea. Just because we are still doing certain things doesn't mean that we should. A college degree is no longer a guarantee. I believe this shift will be felt the most by the students in our K–12 system right now. I know enough to know that we must change the way we are doing things. It won't happen overnight, but we can take small steps to help prepare these young people. Try not to get overwhelmed by the possibilities, and remember each step we take in the right direction gets us closer to that better and brighter future.

Online Resources for Chapter 3

Here you will find resources mentioned in Chapter 3, supplemental resources, videos, as well as new and updated resources.

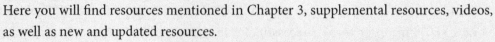

ShakeUpLearningBook.com/3

Discussion Questions

- Does your current curriculum support the entrepreneurial skill set?
- How are you empowering your students to lead and build their own businesses?
- What ideas do you have to cultivate entrepreneurial skills in your classroom?
- What do these entrepreneurial opportunities represent for our students?
- How will entrepreneurial learning change the learning environment?
- What skills do students need to survive in this changing economy?

Chapter 3 Actions

- Watch "Rise of the Entrepreneur," and reflect upon the ideas presented and how it will affect our students (shakeup.link/youtu45e1).
- Explore this Pinterest board of entrepreneurial learning ideas, and brainstorm three ideas for the classroom (shakeup.link/entreb).
- Ask your students about the business ideas and ventures they may already be exploring.

Reflection Space

_____

_____

_____

_____

_____

The Rise of the Entrepreneur

Notes

"Twenty Trends That Will Shape the Next Decade," (*The Intuit 2020 Report*, 2010).

Godin, Seth, *Tribes: We Need You to Lead Us* (New York, NY: Portfolio, 2008).

Newport, Cal, *Deep Work* (New York, NY: Grand Central Publishing, 2016).

Chapter 4
Technology Is Not a Solution

A problem is a terrible thing to waste.
—Peter Diamandis

While technology has changed just about everything in our world and is slowly changing things in our schools, I want to be clear that technology itself is not a solution to the problem. I've seen so many schools invest in technology solutions: going 1:1, putting interactive whiteboards in every room, and investing highly in infrastructure and software applications—while neglecting the needs of the classroom and the classroom teacher. Throwing technology at the various problems we have in our schools will never be a magical solution without purposeful planning aligned with the vision of the school and the learning goals in our classroom—*as well as* ensuring there is meaningful professional development designed for the teacher.

I've seen so many pieces of valuable technology gather dust in the corner of a classroom because the teacher has no idea how to use it or doesn't think it has any use in her subject area or grade level. Even worse, when there are no clear expectations about the use of technology in the school or district itself, you will never see meaningful change. Purpose-driven technology integration can allow us to transform teaching and learning, but it is never a solution all on its own.

In addition, preparing students for the future isn't only about using technology and the latest digital tools. Amid all the advancements we have made in teaching and learning, there are many paths to more meaningful learning that don't use technology at all. Sometimes you really can kick it old-school and still engage students.

When we literally have an app for almost everything, it's hard not to let the apps drive learning in the classroom. Apps are great, but they are not silver bullets. It's what students do with the apps that matter.

Ultimately, schools have spent billions on technology for classrooms, but the investment has not reaped the benefits we hoped to see. Technology in and of itself cannot bring about deeper understanding. There isn't an app for that! Shifting the focus to the tool and the technology is not the right move. Our focus must remain on student learning and leveraging all the tools and strategies at our disposal to transform the learning in our classrooms. Ideally, we want technology to be invisible, seamlessly integrating into classroom activities.

If you follow my blog, you know I frequently share Google-related content. I also have a podcast with my friend, Matt Miller, *The Google Teacher Tribe* (GoogleTeacherTribe.com). Despite the sometimes Google-centric ideas, I am a firm believer in a focus on learning, not tools. In a presentation I've shared at conferences and schools across the country, "It's NOT About Google, It's About the LEARNING," I talk about the International Society for Technology in Education (ISTE) Standards for Students that have a major focus on learning, not tools or how-to skills. Sometimes I do feel like Google can be a gateway drug to technology integration and discovering more tools, and I share how to use Google tools to support these new standards in the classroom. The presentation isn't about Google tools, it's about using these tools to improve student learning.

The key to digital learning is blending what we know about good instruction and assessment with technology to take the entire effort to a new level. It's going beyond what you thought was possible—beyond the worksheet, the tri-fold, and the PowerPoint presentation—and using digital tools for far more than their original purpose. The idea of using new tools to do new things is something I want you to think about, and something we will explore more in-depth in Chapter 8.

I use this example a lot in my teaching. In my early days as an instructional technologist, when document cameras were all the rage and every school was scrambling to get them into classrooms, my district was no different. Part of my job was to instruct teachers how to use them in their classrooms. Most teachers initially saw the "doc cam" as a fancy new overhead projector, but I tried to show them it was so much more. It came with software that allowed you to take pictures, record video of your lessons, and annotate digitally. But the question I heard most often was, "How do I get the glare off the doc cam image when I put my transparency under it?" Yep. You heard me. Teachers were putting their transparencies under the doc cam.

Maybe you were guilty of this as well. But the first time we use any technology, we want to figure out how to use it to do something we have done before—using new technology in old ways. This is obviously just using technology as a substitution, but it is how we learn. While I tried to keep a cool head and understand where these teachers were coming from, I was a bit irritated that they didn't want to use any of the fancy new features I had shown them. They just wanted to know how to use their old transparencies under the new document camera. To prevent glare, many teachers eventually made paper copies of their transparencies and stuck those under the camera. A few tried things the new way. A few used their own money to pay for light bulbs for their old projectors.

Rethinking Assignments

Another common question I receive is about how to upload PDFs to the cloud and annotate or fill them out digitally. Now, I want you to contemplate this carefully. There is always a little gray area, so I try not to immediately assume what the end goal might be. I always follow up with questions of my own to see what type of PDF document they want to use with students. More often than not, teachers want to convert their worksheets to digital worksheets, which is not dynamic at all. This is using new tools to do old things. It's like using twentieth-century logic in twenty-first-century situations. Again, there's a bit of a mindset shift that must take place as you begin to think more dynamically. There may be valuable questions on that PDF, but is it worth giving up the ability to collaborate and create? Can you still integrate any of the Four Cs— critical thinking, communication, collaboration, and/or creativity? We must think differently about the assignments.

As I said, there is always some gray area. I'm sure someone reading this is getting upset about now. That's okay. There are always exceptions. As a reading teacher, I know marking up text is an important skill and even a required skill for some assessments. I'm not saying all PDFs are bad. I just want you to ask yourself a few questions before you decide:

- What is the end goal? What are the learning targets?
- Is this the ONLY approach to teaching this skill or content?
- Are there any ways to integrate the Four Cs?

Now, don't get me wrong, I think there are many reasons to use technology at the substitution level. Right now, I am using Evernote and Google Docs to draft the pages of this book. In many ways, this is still substitution for pen and paper; however, there will be some augmentation used along the way, such as sharing, collaborating, hyperlinking, and good ole spell check.

I received a question from a teacher on social media that really illustrated to me the purpose in rethinking assignments. To protect the innocent, I will summarize the question:

In the past, I've had students create Google Slides presentations and share them with me for a project. This week I assigned the same project and have several students who are showing signs they are probably copying work from former students. How can we prevent this from happening?

The first few answers from followers were revealing. Everyone was focused on the cheating. Cheating was the culprit, the problem. Someone even suggested the teacher stop using tools like Google Slides, where it's so easy to share and copy and paste.

They were focused on the *wrong issue*. Yes, cheating can be a problem, but the problem here was the assignment. The teacher was taking an old assignment, used year after year, something that originated in PowerPoint, and blaming students for copied responses. My response was to think differently about the assignment, because it was as flat as West Texas. If it's something that can be easily duplicated, we need to consider more original product types, incorporate choice of topic and/or tool, and require reflection where they explain their ideas and reflect on learning.

As I pointed out earlier, this book is not a how-to manual for all the latest digital tools. I do offer many resources, tips, tricks, and how-to guides on my blog, *ShakeUpLearning.com*, and I will provide some additional resources and links throughout this book. But if this were an actual how-to book, it would be out of date as soon as it was published. I want to give you more than that.

We need common language and common ground if we are truly going to make a difference and change education. The paradigm shift we've been talking about for years hasn't actually happened yet. We are on the verge but still have many barriers to push through, bad habits to break, and systems to reform. We must make the paradigm shift happen!

An Opportunity for Dynamic Learning

The future is now. It is time to shake up learning! Learning can be completely revolutionized by new technologies if we use them with purpose. We have new ways to differentiate, adapt, and personalize, and we have incredible new ways to collaborate and share our learning. We still might be fighting an antiquated educational system, but we have the resources to transform teaching and learning. Will you embrace it with open arms?

The world we live in is in constant change, a state some describe as dynamic. According to Google Dictionary, a dynamic process or system is characterized by constant change, activity, or progress. I believe the ever-evolving environment in today's classrooms is dynamic as well. To me, the word dynamic is one of the best ways to not only characterize the changes we see in today's world, but also to help us define the new ways to change learning in the classroom. Technological advancements have opened new doors to learning and given us a plethora of new tools to create Dynamic Learning Experiences.

The next step is to shift the way we think about learning. We need to push the boundaries and go *beyond* what we thought was possible and let go of the one-size-fits-all factory model of education that will not prepare our students for the jobs of tomorrow. If we are always giving them boundaries and limits, they will never know what it's like to have limitless learning! The opportunity for dynamic learning is right in front of us. Will you open the door?

Technology is part of almost everything we do, and students expect it. "Kids aren't waiting any longer for someone to tell them what to learn," notes Will Richardson in his TED Talk, "Why School? How Education Must Change When Learning and Information Are Everywhere." They are going to be online and using these devices no matter what, so it's our job to show them how to use technology to navigate the Internet and find reliable sources from which to learn. Our students know how to do all kinds of amazing things online, and we can use those skills to improve their overall learning experience.

These changes must happen now. We must do everything we can to bring education out of the past, and light it up with the power of the future. Let's make sure our students are prepared not only to live in the future, but to lead in the future. That will require radical transformation, and we must look beyond the testing culture that exists in education today. This shift starts with each one of you. Are you ready to create dynamic learning?

Online Resources for Chapter 4

Here you will find resources mentioned in Chapter 4, supplemental resources, videos, as well as new and updated resources.

ShakeupLearningBook.com/4

Discussion Questions

- What opportunities has technology brought to your classroom?
- What problems or barriers keep you from using technology effectively?
- Do you think having one device for every student is ideal? Why or why not?

Chapter 4 Actions

- Make a list of technology to which you (the teacher) have access at school.
- Make a list of technology to which your students have access at school.
- Do you have access to technology in your school that you don't use? Reflect honestly on this question. Circle the ones on your list you don't use.
- Do you have access to technology that you don't know how to use because of lack of training or quality of training? Reflect honestly on this question. Circle the ones on your list.
- After reflecting upon these lists and your own knowledge, what steps can you take to learn more and make the most of what you have?

Reflection Space

_____

_____

_____

_____

_____

_____

_____

_____

_____

_____

_____

_____

_____

_____

_____

_____

_____

_____

_____

Notes

Richardson, Will, "Why School: How Education Must Change When Learning and Information Are Everywhere." *TED Conferences*, 2012.

Part 2

THE WHAT: THE DNA OF DYNAMIC LEARNING

Everything worth building needs a strong foundation, and when it comes to facilitating growth and student learning, we need to insure we have the keys to success. To take learning beyond traditional practices and schooling and move into more Dynamic Learning Experiences, you will need some foundational pedagogy, beliefs, ideas, and skills as a facilitator. Otherwise, what's the point? In this section, we will dive into the DNA of dynamic learning and help prepare you to take action and affect change through your role as an educator.

By taking full advantage of the technological advancements and the changes in learning, we can maximize the academic potential in our classrooms and transition from the fixed activities of yesteryear. I call this dynamic learning.

What Is Dynamic Learning?

Dynamic Learning is learning that goes beyond one-and-done activities and allows the learning to live and grow by providing learning experiences that break the bounds of the school day and classroom walls, taking us beyond due dates and prescribed curriculums, and redefining the use of digital tools. It's like giving your classroom metabolism a boost! (We will go much deeper into this definition in Chapter 14.)

In the next few chapters, we will explore the foundational principals of dynamic learning: risk-taking, breaking barriers and bad habits, and the importance of connecting, always learning, sharing your voice, unleashing creative thinking, going global, and empowering students.

Chapter 5

Get Comfortable with Being Uncomfortable

Courage is not the absence of fear;
it is pressing forward when you feel afraid.
—Joyce Meyer

At the heart of big changes usually lie big risks. You must get comfortable with being uncomfortable—especially if you plan to go beyond the bounds of traditional learning. Risk-taking is a hot topic, and it's easy and often fun to talk about doing it. It's a whole other feeling to put yourself out on a limb and buck the status quo.

Are you uncomfortable yet? I want to make you uncomfortable. I know that sounds strange, but comfort is my enemy. The comfort zone is enemy territory. Do you know someone who is too comfortable in their role as a teacher? The moment I feel comfortable, I know it's time to find a new challenge. It's my job to push teachers out of their comfort zones, so I am doing teachers a disservice if I don't push them—or even drag them—into the twenty-first century.

So get uncomfortable. Get really uncomfortable! The only way to know what you and your students are truly capable of is to push your limits. Place your bets, take the risk, and learn like you are in Vegas! Taking a risk during the learning process is a gamble, but one that can pay off big time. Taking a risk in the classroom might not end in the success you predicted, but if truly done with purpose, the process can reap valuable learning along the way.

The *F* Word

Fear. Some folks call it "the other *F* word." However you think of it, fear is powerful. It can literally stop us in our tracks. Sometimes that's a good thing. Fear can keep us safe, making us aware of danger or inhibiting stupid decisions we'd later regret. Fear also tends to spike when we're simply trying out a new environment or skill, and in those cases, it can be difficult to face and conquer. I guarantee most educators who want to innovate, push boundaries, and challenge the status quo grapple with fears of failure and rejection. They also press on because they believe they can make a difference. Do you believe you can make a difference? I do.

The best success stories always have a bottom. Some of the most successful people in the world have failed their way to the top. Failure isn't the opposite of success. It's a necessary part of

FOCUS ON WHAT MATTERS

At this point you might be thinking, "Isn't good pedagogy at the heart of teaching and learning?" And is it just me, or is anyone else tired of the word "pedagogy" and arguing about how to pronounce it? It's a word that often gets convoluted and watered down. What does it actually mean? Many articles have been written debating that very topic, and that is certainly not the point of this book, which is meant to be much more practical. For our purposes, we will define pedagogy as *the process of bringing learning to life*. Isn't that what it's all about? Don't get caught up in old-school vernacular when we are trying to push the boundaries, break bad habits, and redefine what learning can be. Let's focus on what matters—student learning—and how to use everything at our disposal to bring it to life.

Be careful not to escort your students directly through the path that leads to success. Let them discover it, even if their path is different from one you might take. Your role is to encourage, ask thought-provoking questions, and help students to recognize success. This is why project- and problem-based learning is so critical. They offer room to grow, make mistakes, correct course, and create. Daily one-and-done activities are not enough to shake up learning. Your classroom must be more dynamic, and we'll discuss more on this in Chapter 6.

I have always loved this concept of failing forward. It almost seems counter-intuitive, but it makes perfect sense. Yes, risk-taking is scary. Yes, sometimes administrators do not support our risks. But without failing forward or failing our way to the top, we will never reach our potential as educators, and our students will never learn how to use their own failures to grow and learn.

I love the image below. It's simple and one you might have seen before, but it is so profound. What can you do to step outside your comfort zone and make the magic happen?

FIGURE 5.1

success. We must consider each failure a stepping stone. How many times have you started a project and had to start over because your approach was all wrong? This happens to me all the time. But you know what? I rarely make that mistake again.

The hard part is letting go. It can be difficult for teachers to step back and give students room to fail, but if we're there to catch them every time, they're not learning to do it on their own.

Most of us agree our educational system is broken, and standardized tests are not the answer. The reality is that most real-world problems do not have one correct answer, and failure often means different things to educators and students. I frequently use the FAIL acronym—First Attempt in Learning—in my teaching and workshops. A curriculum director once asked me to remove that acronym from the website we were using because the word *fail*, I was told, had no place in that school district. She didn't get it, y'all. For her, the word *fail* was too closely associated with performance on a standardized test to be viewed in any other way. Some educators and administrators are wearing blinders when it comes to doing what's best for kids. And who's to say learning to take risks and different approaches to problem-solving can't lead to better understanding and a passing grade on the test? I don't think it's a choice. Teachers are doing their students a disservice if those students graduate only with good test-taking strategies.

If you want to be creative, you must be willing to take risks! Better yet, if you want your students to tap into their creativity, you must encourage and facilitate risk-taking in your classroom.

My story, which I shared at the beginning of this book, was really just a story about taking risks. I have had plenty of failures along the way, and each time I learned a valuable lesson that helped me better understand the problem and gain new perspectives. You cannot fix what you cannot face. The courage to take risks in learning can reveal new depths of understanding in a way that answering questions on a worksheet never can.

Model Risk-taking for Your Students

The magic happens outside of your comfort zone. Don't be afraid to step out and model risk-taking in your classroom. Let your students know when you fail or make a mistake so they will come to see it's a normal part of life. Find ways to push students out of their comfort zones, give them new ideas and perspectives, and teach them how to see the value in failing forward. Discuss famous failures such as Steve Jobs, Abraham Lincoln, and Michael Jordan, and dig into how many times it took for them to get it right.

If you have been playing it safe during your teaching career, I challenge you to get uncomfortable. In the words of one of my favorite Texas country artists, "Am I crazy enough?" Don't be afraid of being known as "that crazy teacher" who's always trying new ideas. Be crazy enough to transform your classroom, to be dynamic, and to be the teacher everyone is always talking about. To really take action on the ideas presented in this book, you need to be prepared to fall flat on your face. Are you ready? You will never know what you and your students are capable of if you don't step out of your comfort zone. Try something new today that makes you uncomfortable.

Ask Better Questions

To support students who are taking risks and possibly making what they perceive as mistakes, we must carefully consider the questions we ask. Do the questions you ask have right and wrong answers? Is there only one way to complete the problem? Real-world problems don't have one correct answer.

How are mistakes treated in your classroom? The students who often raise their hand to answer a question, usually are confident that they know the correct answer. A lot of students are terrified of blundering. These fears keep students from participating in discussion, trying something new, coloring outside the lines, and thinking in a different way. Because success in school is often measured by how well you do on a test, mistakes have not played a positive role. How can we create a safe environment for students to join in the discussion even when they aren't sure of the answer? Better yet, can we ask better questions and give students better problems to solve?

As Sir Ken Robinson tells us in his popular TED Talk, "Do Schools Kill Creativity?," students have been programmed to think there is one correct answer. It's located in the back of the book, and if you look, that's cheating. But what if we asked questions that don't have just one correct answer? Is there a book on life that contains correct answers to all of life's questions? If so, let me know.

I am often asked some variation of "How do I lock down a computer to one tab during a quiz so my students can't open new tabs and Google the answers?"

My answer usually goes something like, "Why not give them questions that they can't do a Google search for?" Meaning, can you ask more in-depth questions that require creative thinking as opposed to an answer that will appear at the top of a Google search? Yes, there are skills and concepts students need to learn that only have one answer but should not be the focus on every learning experience.

Why are we spending valuable time, energy, and money locking down access to information in our schools—of all places—ignoring the real world, and pretending it doesn't exist? What good will that do our students? Guess what I do when I don't know the answer? I do a Google search for it. Just like you do.

If we want students to understand real-world problems, they need to understand there isn't just one correct answer. We need to ask more insightful, provocative questions—the kind that don't have their answer listed in the back of the book. How can you help develop students who are inquisitive problem solvers? Resist the urge to feed them answers. Feed them questions!

It's time for your Popeye moment! I grew up on Popeye the Sailorman, and in every episode Popeye faced his fears with the help of a heaping dose of spinach. Popeye put up with a lot— Bluto kicking him around and trying to steal his precious Olive Oyl—until he couldn't take it anymore. I believe his exact words were, "That's all I can stands. I can't stands no more!" Well it's time that we as teachers "can't stands no more"! I hope some of the ideas in this book can serve as your spinach, your secret strength to step out of the comfy and take action! (For fun, watch this throwback to see Popeye and his spinach in action: shakeup.link/youtu120e.)

Are you ready for your Popeye moment? Don't let the *F* word hold you back from trying new things. Embrace your fears and be a model risktaker for other educators and students and help your students to fail forward.

IS IT WORTH IT FOR ME TO STEP INTO MY FEARS?

TAKE THE LEAP!

☐ **YES!** Making the magic happen in my classroom is worth it!

☐ No, I'd rather stay stuck in my comfort zone.

LET'S DO THIS!

Online Resources for Chapter 5

Here you will find resources mentioned in Chapter 5, supplemental resources, videos, as well as new and updated resources.

ShakeUpLearningBook.com/5

Discussion Questions

- How do you create a culture of risk-taking in the classroom? How do you react when your students don't grasp a concept or skill the first time you teach it?
- What opportunities do you give students to take risks?
- How are you modeling risk-taking?
- Are you providing long-term learning experiences that give students the opportunity to create their own path toward the learning goals? If not, what are some long-term learning experiences you would like to try?
- What opportunities have you avoided because of self-imposed limitations?

Chapter 5 Actions

- Think about a risk you have been avoiding. It could be personal or professional. Be honest and write down what is truly holding you back. Now write down what the possible payoff could be. Ready to move forward? Create a list of steps to accomplish this goal and get moving!
- Start a discussion in your classroom about risk-taking. What kind of learning risks are okay? Do students feel comfortable sharing and asking questions when they are unsure of the answer?
- Model something new for your students that you have never tried before. Let them know you aren't sure if it will work and that you are taking a risk.
- Have a "Failing Forward Day" dedicated to stepping out and trying new things in the classroom. Use this to help build a culture of risk-taking in the classroom.

Reflection Space

→ ◯Chapter 6 →→→
Breaking Barriers and Bad Habits

If school's function is to create the workers we need to fuel our economy, we need to change school, because the workers we need have changed as well.
—Seth Godin

As discussed in Chapter 2, the world has changed in profound ways, and along with that evolution have come changes to the way we learn. Change is coming to education, slowly but surely. The skills needed to survive in this new and ever-changing economy are different than the skills needed by our grandparents and great-grandparents.

Dynamic learning requires that we let go of the traditional ideas that we have about school and education. In fact, I bet many of you began to think of the policies in your school that could be a barrier to the ideas presented so far. There are also some things we do in our classrooms and in our schools that are just habits or requirements, and no one seems to question their purpose or how they affect student learning. Are the barriers and bad habits a necessary evil? If they are truly barriers to learning and transforming education, shouldn't we do something? Are you doing your part to break down walls and stop playing games?

The Game of School

Change is coming . . . In the game of school, we change, or students lose.

For many educators and students, school has become a game. By the time students reach the middle grades, they have either mastered the game, or they haven't. Unfortunately, this game has become so ingrained in our systems and testing, it can be hard to see your own contributions to the game. To break these barriers and bad habits, we must stop playing. Real learning can happen anytime, anywhere, and it is driven by personalization, interests, passions, and curiosity, not by the one-size-fits-all compliance model that seems to be the ruling factor in many U.S. schools.

I learned to play the game of school very well. I was a traditional learner. I could listen to lectures, take notes, and please my teachers with most of my work. I made it through with good grades only because I mastered the rules of the game of school—turning in work (usually worksheets) on time. I didn't lose points for behavior, late work, or other non-learning related point reductions. I even collected extra credit for bringing in a couple of boxes of Kleenex and poster board. But guess what? I didn't learn much at all and wasn't remotely prepared for the challenges of college. The problem was, I hadn't actually learned how to learn. My first few years as a classroom teacher, I didn't function all that differently from the teachers of my childhood. I taught the way I had been taught, graded the way I had been graded, and I created many bad habits.

Why? The best answer I have is that most schools offer a one-size-fits-all experience, and I was a product of that environment. I now realize that approach falls short. It might meet the standards and result in diplomas being awarded, but it's not truly serving students. Think about it: Schools all over the country continue every day with policies that adversely affect learning. Why do we create all these little boxes and try to fit each student into an assigned learning space? In some schools, students aren't even allowed to interact with students in different boxes! We are still churning out millions of workers who are trained to be compliant factory workers of the twentieth century.

Consider our day-to-day schedules. Why do we create the schedule first and then decide how to make time for the learning? Why doesn't the learning drive the schedule? You can't schedule greatness! And why do we grade behaviors? Shouldn't grading reflect actual learning and mastery? Why do some teachers present lessons the same way year after year? They're certainly not teaching the same kids every year. Maybe we do these things because they're working, but I suspect it's because that's just the way it has always been done. It's not our fault we played the game. To quote Ice-T, "Don't hate the playa, hate the game." We can and must do better.

Are You Playing the Game of School?

Have you ever thought about how the way you grade and assess work or how the way you are required to grade could be contributing to the game of school? There have been many articles, books, and theories on shifting the way we assess and assign grades. The bottom line is a grade on a report card should be reflective of learning, not whether little Sally was compliant and submitted her work on time.

Extra credit tends to play a major role in the secondary world. I remember those students who were always on the edge of a failing grade and needed an extra boost to bring them up. Sometimes the coaches sent them out to the teachers during the last week of the six-week grading period to basically beg for extra credit assignments. I couldn't tell you if those students acquired any new knowledge or skills through the extra credit work. In Joy Kirr's book, *Shift This*, she says, "If the work assigned is not something you'd let them redo in order to learn, it's time to assess the relevance of the work you're assigning." Some teachers would give extra credit points for bringing in supplies like Kleenex, pencils, or poster board. In exchange for partial credit, students were sometimes given a chance to complete an assignment they had never turned in. At what point do grades actually reflect learning and not just how well students are at negotiating with teachers and playing the game of school?

I've even worked for administrators who told me I was required to deduct or add a certain percentage of points based on behavior. Gasp if you will, but this practice is still happening. The system is perpetuated every day.

In fact, I have been part of the problem. I used to keep a stack of homework passes in my desk. Yes, I did! There were a lot of ways I played the game of school, both as a student and as a teacher. Those homework passes became very valuable to my students. By behaving well for a substitute when I was away, my students could cash in their homework passes on any assignment they wished without doing any of the work or demonstrating any learning. The fact that I did that still hurts my heart. I didn't think about the disservice I was doing my students. Their grades were much more of a reflection of behavior and compliance than they were of actual learning or achievement.

In some of my previous schools, we also had late-work policies to dictate how many points a student would lose based on how late the work was submitted. I know this practice is still commonplace in many schools. It's all part of the game. Don't get me wrong—turning in work on time is a life skill, but it should be part of a behavior management system and not tied to a letter grade, a grade point average, or a student's ultimate success in school or beyond. To any former students now reading this book, please accept my apologies for playing

the game of school. I wish I'd known better. None of us are perfect, but we can improve and make a difference.

If you're an educator who's re-evaluating your contribution to the game of school, take a moment to reflect on your everyday tasks. Are there systems in place that are more about pushing students to be compliant instead of supporting their learning? Rethink the purpose of grades in your class and in your school. Above all, the grades you issue should reflect learning and achievement.

Are We Stuck?

Are we stuck? Are you stuck? Are you afraid of what your principal will say? Are you afraid you will get into trouble? Playing the game of school is playing it safe, and there's no way to come out winning if you always play it safe. Our students lose! Fear of change is built into the culture of the factory model. But what if companies like AOL hadn't played it safe? Where might they be right now?

Is education stable or stuck—or both? We cannot make assumptions and pretend this way of educating students is actually working or that it will work in the future. If we keep teaching the way we've always taught, this country will drown.

I once heard a story about a woman who grew up in a large, poor family. They didn't have much to eat. When this woman got married and cooked

> Change is coming… In the game of school, we change, or students lose.

for her new husband, she took one can of soup and watered it down with five cans of water. The new husband asked her why she did that for a meal intended for only two people? She replied, "That's the way my mother did it." She knew she wasn't feeding seven people anymore and didn't need to water down the soup, but that way of living had become a habit. How many decisions are made in schools or about education in general because that's the way it has always been done? At some point, these decisions were likely necessary and served a purpose, but now they don't make sense. Always question why things are done the way they are done.

The game of school goes much deeper than what was discussed here, but I just want to spark the conversation and get you thinking. I think most of us agree the educational system in the United States is broken, but most of us don't think it is our duty to change it. We leave it up to the others, the advocates, the lobbyists, the lawmakers, and that's why nothing has changed. The problem doesn't lie in only one area—it's systemic. But we can't simply pass the time as bystanders. We must be upstanders if we want to see change.

I believe that change starts with you. Start small and think of the bad habits you may have formed that are contributing to the game of school. Start with your classroom or your role in education. Every small step will take us closer to meaningful change. If you want something to change, you must be willing to stand up and fight for those changes. Challenge the status quo! Create change you believe in. Be a game-changer, not a player!

Online Resources for Chapter 6

Here you will find resources mentioned in Chapter 6, supplemental resources, videos, as well as new and updated resources.

ShakeUpLearningBook.com/6

Discussion Questions

- What things need to change in your classroom to make it less of a one-size-fits-all experience?
- In what ways do you need to stop playing along with the game of school?
- In your classroom, how do grades reflect learning?

Chapter 6 Actions

- Start small. Brainstorm the tasks you do every day in your role as an educator. How do these tasks contribute to student learning? How do they contribute to the game? Pick one thing you can challenge or change.
- Start a discussion in your school or district about things that need to change. Start small and keep a positive tone. Start with yourself and what you can do right now. Post a reflection online to spark the conversation.

Reflection Space

Notes

Kirr, Joy, *Shift This* (San Diego, CA: Dave Burgess Consulting, Inc., 2017).

Chapter 7
Always Be Learning

The most important skill to teach students in the
age of the Internet is to learn how to learn.
—Alan November

As I have mentioned before, teachers are my students, and I am often asked to do a lot of handholding and offer step-by-step instructions for every little task. But I try to resist doing too much coddling because things change so fast. Even if I wrote a detailed comparison of Google Drive, Dropbox, and Office 365 to help teachers understand the differences in these products and select the right one for their campus or organization, by the time I completed my research, some part of it likely would be out of date. It happens to me all the time. I'll create a blog post to show a Google tip, and the next day or next week, Google releases an update that makes my post invalid and out of date. I'm not saying I don't still try to give teachers the step-by-step when possible, but I prefer to teach teachers and students how to fish for their own answers.

I believe the best skill I can give my students is the ability to teach themselves and to find the answers to their questions on their own. For instance, in my blog series, "The Guide to Keeping Up with Google," I provide blogs, social media accounts, YouTube channels, and more to help educators keep up with the changes and learn

as they go. In my presentations, I focus on ways to use technology and digital tools to streamline procedures, increase productivity, and, of course, the countless ways to use them in the K–12 classroom. I also did a post called "Gone App Fishing: Finding the Best Apps for Your Classroom." This is a post with a similar idea where I listed websites, blogs, and apps to help teachers find the best apps, vetted with reviews, for their classroom instead of relying on random Google searches.

Do you know how to fish for your own resources? As Felix Jacomino, the director of innovation and technology at Gulliver Schools in Miami, Florida, said during a presentation I attended at iPadpalooza, "Give a teacher an app, and she's got a day's lesson. Teach her how to find the right apps, and she'll have lessons for a lifetime." By fishing, I don't mean simply Googling for the answer and then moving on. Sometimes a Google Search is the worst place to start. It's important to know how to use Google Advanced searches, support pages, forums, trusted bloggers, YouTube channels, and your entire personal learning network to help you find the best help and resources for your task. Most of all, students and teachers need to develop a mindset of continuous learning. Learning how to learn is one of the most important skills they can acquire to thrive in today's world. School is sometimes viewed as a one-and-done kind of accomplishment, but if we want our students to be successful in future endeavors, including running their own businesses, we must show them the power of teaching themselves. And we should focus on all kinds of learning, not just the how-to of mastering a specific program or tool. Entrepreneurs especially need to be ahead of the curve, developing their own original concepts and not just learning how to apply the ideas of others. Don't you dare trade your calling as a teacher for something that is one and done.

Resist the urge to Google things for other people, especially students. It isn't doing them any favors. Show them how to do it on their own. This also applies to professional development. Taking ownership of your own professional learning at all stages is critical, and it's a skill that should be modeled and passed on to our students. Technology is only going to continue to change—and change rapidly. If you aren't willing to find your own answers, troubleshoot your own problems, find a YouTube video to teach you how, or click around and figure it out on your own, you should consider another field. The days of being spoon-fed information are over, both in training for teachers, and for instruction in our classrooms. Give your students the skills they need to fish throughout their lives.

Consider your classroom. How do you encourage students to take the initiative to learn things on their own, to find answers to their own questions and problems? Do you show your students how to take ownership, ask meaningful questions, and ask for help? With multiple forms of communication at our fingertips, we can easily encourage students to use tools such as messaging in Google Hangouts, comments, and social media to communicate with us, other teachers, their classmates, and experts outside of class.

Are you using Google searches as teachable moments? Show students how to filter and refine their results to find answers. Show them how to use support pages and forums. Show them how to decipher advertising from valid sources. Help students learn how to learn and teach themselves new skills.

Google for Education offers some great resources for teachers and students to improve their search skills with Google Search Education. Here you will find lesson plans for all skill levels, challenges, advanced tips, and even some free training. (See chapter resources for links.)

One of the most obvious innovations in learning is the use of video. Video learning is easily accessed, easy to use, and wildly popular. You can learn how to do just about anything on YouTube! I bet you have learned something from YouTube. Where do your students go when they want to learn how to do something? YouTube. How are you making use of this resource for your own learning and for that of your students?

I talk a lot about Google Certifications and how much I have learned through each one of my certifications. If you are looking to up your Google game, pursue a certification! Even if you aren't that concerned with getting certified, the Google for Education Training Center (edutrainingcenter.withgoogle.com) offers a great way to teach yourself some new skills. If you are interested in certification, I have a ton of free resources on my blog to help you on your journey.

I'm pretty good at teaching, but I am really good at learning and teaching myself new skills. That's how I developed a knack for this technology thing. Those of us who work in the education-technology realm are mostly good at learning, finding answers, and troubleshooting. We are not experts in everything, but we have a knack for solving problems. It's this skill that I believe we must pass on to our students.

Online Resources for Chapter 7

Here you will find resources mentioned in Chapter 7, supplemental resources, videos, as well as new and updated resources.

ShakeupLearningBook.com/7

Discussion Questions

- How do you keep up with the changes to your favorite digital tools? How do you learn about new strategies and digital tools?
- How do you learn new skills?
- How do you encourage students to teach themselves when they don't know how to do something?

Chapter 7 Actions

- Create a learning experience that requires students to solve problems and teach themselves a new skill. Use change as a catalyst for learning.
- Teach yourself a new skill by watching a YouTube video. Maybe you've always wanted to learn how to use Google Classroom, or maybe you want to know how to make awesome YouTube tutorials? I guarantee you will find something useful on YouTube. If you aren't sure where to start, check out my YouTube channel and playlists at youtube.com/c/KaseyBell.
- *18 Challenges for Teachers in 2018* (FREE eBook) (shakeup.link/18challenges)—This is an eBook I created at the beginning of 2018 to challenge teachers to learn and try new things. Take a gander and try something on this list.

Reflection Space

Chapter 8
Uberize Your Learning and Curate Resources

*We're assembling resources in a way that represents the
ongoing story of our learning. We are the curators.*
—Gayle Allan

As I mentioned earlier, learning has changed a lot in the past 150 years, especially in the past decade. With the rise in entrepreneurship, online learning, social media, and packaged digital content, anyone can learn just about anything online. Free and paid sources for learning, including online degrees, micro-credentials and certifications, email courses, YouTube videos, online courses, and presentations, are at our disposal around the clock. Learning has gone public and à la carte! Just about anyone can learn what they want at just the time they need it. I like to think of this as a way to Uberize your learning.

Uber has turned the transportation industry on its heels. They have crowd-sourced rides to and from just about anywhere. It's far from a perfect system, but fifteen years ago, who among us thought we would ever jump into a car with a stranger to get from one place to the next? Who thought we would pay strangers online for content, eBooks, courses, tutorials, and teaching materials? This is the shift we are seeing in the world, and to ignore the impact of this shift in the realm of K–12 education would be a dire mistake.

Today the abundance of information and resources requires that we curate, whether that's taking notes, bookmarking, Pinterest boards, or another preferred tool. Many tools now offer ways to take the searching out of the equation and deliver suggested resources directly to you. The content can come to us, much like the arrival of an Uber driver at a desired location and time, and give us the option to customize or upgrade the ride to fit our needs. Blog subscriptions, Pinterest feeds, Facebook stream, and shares from your curated PLN are just a few of the ways to Uberize your learning.

If you follow my blog, you know I curate a lot of resources for teachers. Curation is absolutely necessary in the information age! As Gayle Allen says in her book, *The New Pillars of Modern Teaching*, "We're assembling resources in a way that represents the ongoing story of our learning. We are the curators." Curation takes time. It can take a lot of time, and that's why I share so many curated resources on my website. Your time is valuable. Curating on your own is great. Collaboratively curating is even better. Following bloggers and feeds that deliver resources to your (virtual) door—the best!

As you are reading this book, you might encounter some resources you want to save or bookmark. Some of you might be taking paper notes and writing everything down. That's okay! Do what works for you, but I want to encourage you to try some digital curation. That piece of paper can't follow you and be there whenever you need it. Digital notes, links, bookmarks, and curation tools can help you find what you need the second you need it and from any device.

If you have jumped on the social media bandwagon, you have probably saved, liked, and favorited countless resources, but do you have a system for searching this collection and finding the specific one you want?

Digital bookmarking can make life so much easier. For a simple start, just bookmark resources in your browser. I prefer Google Chrome because my bookmarks are saved to the cloud, and I can access that content from any device.

I use a digital bookmarking tool called Diigo (www.diigo.com). I have used Diigo for several years. That's a pretty good life for a digital tool to stick around! Diigo allows me to bookmark resources such as websites and add notes, tags, and even annotations like highlighting an important quote on the screen. Even better, I can then share my bookmarks, notes, and annotations with others. You can also create groups on Diigo and share content directly with the group or your class.

Another favorite tool for curation and notes is Google Keep (keep.google.com). Here you can add notes, to-do lists, reminders, voice notes, images, and much more. There's a handy Google Keep Chrome extension that allows you to easily add a web resource into your Google Keep Notepad. I could probably write an entire chapter on this amazing tool, but I will instead refer you to the resources section for this chapter so you can learn more and curate your own resources!

I mentioned YouTube as a great resource for learning new skills, but it becomes even more powerful when you add videos to curated playlists. If you visit my channel playlists, you will see I curate not only my own videos into playlists but also videos from other sources. When a teacher asks me a question about a certain topic, I can give them a link to a playlist of tutorials. How awesome is that? You can easily use YouTube to curate a playlist for a topic, unit of study, or tutorials to help students. Think of the ways you can use YouTube in your classroom to curate videos for your students.

One of my favorite curation tools is Pinterest. Pinterest is a visual bookmarking tool, where users save bookmarks or "pins" onto their virtual boards to organize and revisit. Pinterest is also a powerful search engine. (You don't even need an account to search.) Use it to find and discover new ideas for the classroom or for your home and your life. It has become particularly popular among educators. I find a lot of amazing lesson ideas and educational resources on Pinterest. I promise Pinterest isn't just for crafting and recipes. And to those who think it is just for women, you are mistaken. It's a great resource and curation tool for anyone. Don't believe me? Check out my Pinterest boards at www.pinterest.com/ShakeUpLearning. Pinterest is a great space to find and curate ideas for your classroom.

Uberize Your Learning and Curate Resources

Gayle Allen reminds us curation is not just a valuable skill for teachers. It can equip students to navigate the busy world that awaits them. "Curation skills help them manage and maximize the information coming at them each day," she says.

When students learn to curate, it eases the burden on teachers to be the keeper of all knowledge and resources. Students might know how to take a screenshot of a Snap from SnapChat, but do they know how to save important learning resources to access at a later date?

I encourage you to find ways to demonstrate and model curation—share a video playlist with your students—and build curation into the learning experiences in your classroom. Research is a natural fit for curation, but there are many reasons to use this skill in more informal manners. We have no shortage of resources these days, but finding valid, reliable information and having it ready at our fingertips can save teachers and students time and frustration. It's a fun, relevant way to empower students and give them ownership of their learning.

Online Resources for Chapter 8

Here you will find resources mentioned in Chapter 8, supplemental resources, videos, as well as new and updated resources.

ShakeupLearningBook.com/8

Discussion Questions

- How are you Uberizing your learning and finding new resources?
- How do you curate resources for yourself and your students?
- What curation strategy or tool would you like to try?

Chapter 8 Actions

- If you have not been digitally curating resources, try something new, whether it's bookmarking in your browser or curating on Diigo, YouTube, or Pinterest.
- Create a YouTube playlist for a learning experience in your classroom (three or more videos).
- Create a Pinterest account, and create a board with lesson ideas on one specific topic.
- Research other curation tools, and find what works for you!
- Create an experience for students to learn at least one way to curate resources for learning.

Reflection Space

_____

_____

_____

_____

_____

_____

_____

_____

_____

_____

_____

Notes

Allen, Gayle, *The New Pillars of Modern Teaching* (Bloomington, IN: Solution Tree Press, 2015).

Chapter 9
Unleash Creative Thinking

An innovative culture never happens by accident.
You have to create a creative culture.
—Craig Groeschel

reativity is vastly becoming one of the most important skills of the twenty-first century. In fact, Sir Ken Robinson says, "Creativity is as important as literacy." We need students who are prepared for jobs that are not based on a one-size-fits-all model. These jobs will require not only creativity and innovation but also a willingness to embrace the messy and the chaotic. To prepare our students for this kind of work, we must allow them to tackle a little mess and a little chaos in the classroom. When things get messy—and I'm not talking glitter and glue—teachers must dive in and become facilitators of the messy. I'm talking about allowing creativity to flourish, bubble over, and spawn elevated noise, laughing, music, debates, and all those other things that can get a classroom unfairly judged as chaotic and out of control. Our students must be allowed and taught to learn, work, and solve problems within this chaos because it is the world they face.

Seth Godin reminds us in his TEDxYouth talk *Stop Stealing Dreams* that when it comes to work, people naturally try to figure out how to do less, and if it's art, we try to figure out how to do more. And this is how students are programmed to react to school "work." I had some students, a lot but not all, who always tried to figure out the easiest way to complete the assignment, cutting every corner. They weren't engaged, and they were not unleashing creativity.

Most teachers like structure, and with good reason. Structure in the classroom is necessary, especially for many learners, but overly structured classes can stifle creativity. Sometimes students grow too dependent on structure and expect to be given a formula for every activity. I found this was especially true for my advanced students. These students had learned to the play the game of school, much like I had, and they wanted to know which path would lead to an A, and that was all that mattered. So when faced with more authentic learning experiences requiring messy, out-of-the-box thinking, these advanced students floundered. In fact, they usually needed more hand-holding when I told them there was more than one way to complete the assignment and demonstrate their learning.

When we think about the future workforce and the jobs our students will have, we come up with one giant question mark. The world is advancing so quickly that we can't predict the trends, but we do know jobs that can be automated by artificial intelligence, robots, formulas, and algorithms will be taken over by machines.

One Correct Answer

In the game of school, students are taught there is one way, one correct answer, one path to success, and this type of thinking is the absolute opposite of creativity and innovation. Creativity can take a million different forms and mediums and lead us in completely unexpected directions. But how in the world do you teach creativity?

I was told for many years that creativity needed to be a part of my classroom, but nobody handed me the textbook on creativity and said, "This is how you do it." That's because creativity cannot be contained in something as mundane and structured as a textbook. You can't teach creativity; you unleash it! Sometimes this means teachers simply need to get out of the way. We need to step back, give students room to explore, stretch their creative legs, and make a few mistakes. It can be difficult to keep such distance, especially when you are used to feeding students information and guiding them onto a problem-solving path. But remember that learning can happen in the messiness. When discussing ideas with your students, encourage and challenge by asking more provocative questions. Help them see the bigger picture, the real-world connections, the cultural connections, the artistic connections, and to question each other. Give your students opportunities to be creative at all levels!

Exemplars can also stifle creativity. If students are told there is only one correct answer or one way to complete an activity or project, they will follow that formula. Creativity isn't formulaic. Creativity is spontaneous and amorphous and fluid! Guidance is great, but I have discovered, no matter the age of the students, when you show them an example of a completed project, they want to replicate it. That kind of learning leaves little room for creativity. Most real-world problems do not have one correct answer or come with examples of possible solutions.

To better illustrate this theory, I'd like to introduce you to an interesting YouTube video, "When There Is a Correct Answer," from the Rama School and Elad Segev. In this video, third-grade students were given directions that included a simple triangle and were told to "complete the painting." Students were told those who completed the painting "the right way" would receive one point. Almost all the students turned their triangles into the roof of a house. Nice work, but not too creative. The same students were given the assignment again with new instructions. They were given a triangle and told to "complete the painting." This time, however, they were not told a correct answer would be rewarded with points. The more open-ended assignment resulted in new ideas. The second paintings told stories, created robots, monsters, and traveled to foreign lands. This time, their creativity was unleashed!

When students were told there was a right way to complete the painting, 80 percent drew a house, and the average number of colors used was just two. In contrast, when students were simply told to complete the painting, they used their imaginations freely. Apologies for the pun, but too much structure can paint students into a box! Are you willing to be a facilitator of the messy?

Like most skills, facilitating the messy takes practice—on the part of teachers and students. The first time I gave students a little bit of creative freedom in my classroom, they thought it would be a one-and-done activity. They were also very concerned about doing it wrong. We want our students to practice and develop their learning in the chaos of collaboration, discussion, and creation. We want our students to develop a habit of creativity.

Adults also have a tough time with creative tasks. Today, teachers are my students, and whenever I give them freedom in professional learning activities, they panic. They want to know which tool is the right tool to use, or how long it has to be, or they want to see the correct example. (Some even ask if they have to write in complete sentences!) It's hard to make this shift as a teacher and as a learner. Baby steps will help students see the path to creative freedom.

I know creativity is not a part of our state assessments or on a bubble sheet, but the culture must shift, and if we don't help our students tap into these skills, we are doing them a disservice. Kids deserve so much more than test-taking skills and the knowledge to formalize correct answers. Our time is better served helping students find their own answers or create new ones instead of just memorizing the one correct answer. The most innovative minds of the past one hundred years were disruptive—yes, they were shaking things up! Creative problem-solving requires that students believe they can find a solution and do something about it. Every problem, real or simulated, presents us with hidden opportunities to be innovative. Help your students get messy with meaning and purpose. Embrace the chaos and learn with them. Facilitate the messy in your classroom!

Online Resources for Chapter 9

Here you will find resources mentioned in Chapter 9, supplemental resources, videos, as well as new and updated resources.

ShakeupLearningBook.com/9

Discussion Questions

- How do you encourage creativity and innovation? How do you foster it as a teacher?
- Where are the opportunities for creativity and innovative problem-solving in your classroom?
- How can you be less rigid in your assignments and facilitate the messiness of creativity?
- What would happen if you gave students the freedom to demonstrate their learning in their own way, using whatever tools they want?

Chapter 9 Actions

- Revise a rigid lesson that you do every year with more flexibility and opportunities to be creative.
- Try the "Complete the Painting" activity with your students. You might be surprised what skills this could unlock.

Reflection Space

_____

_____

_____

_____

_____

_____

_____

_____

_____

Notes

Robinson, Ken, "Do Schools Kill Creativity?" *TED*, 2006, www.ted.com/talks/ken_robinson_says_schools_kill_creativity.

Chapter 10
Connect and Share

*The first step to connect your classroom to
the world is to connect yourself first.*
—Vicki Davis

The social technology context of our world cannot be ignored. It's in our face every day. It has had and will have an even greater influence over our students and future students. Many teachers fail to see the value of collaborating and sharing their learning online, but this mode of connecting has truly become essential. It's simply the way the world learns these days.

This big world of ours is getting smaller. With applications like Facebook, Twitter, SnapChat, Instagram, Pinterest, Tumblr, and WhateverNewAppisComingOutofSiliconValley, we can follow just about anyone or anything that interests us. These platforms give us the tools to show our students the world beyond the walls of the classroom. Social media, and Twitter in particular, allows us to connect and build relationships with total strangers. We can cultivate amazing friendships and close-knit relationships with people who follow us. In many cases, followers equal influence. If anyone tells you any different, they are lying. This means individuals, anyone for that matter, can have far more power and influence than ever before.

We live in a world where one YouTube video can create a pop star overnight, a careless Tweet can cause you to lose your job or even go to jail, one Snap can create a party or a flash mob, a single Instagram post can organize a protest, a Facebook post can broadcast a murder live to the world. One person has the power to do just about anything. Think of what this means for our students! We need to use this power to elevate student learning.

Erik Qualman has written three phenomenal books on the topic of social media: *Socialnomics, What Happens in Vegas Stays on YouTube,* and *What Happens on Campus Stays on YouTube.* All contain some eye-opening realities. In his book *What Happens in Vegas Stays on YouTube,* Qualman points out that privacy is dead, and reputations are dying. He argues that we must turn this potential liability into leadership opportunities.

According to Qualman, common sense is not that common, and we should live as if our mother is watching. We all will make mistakes, and one in three people regret something they posted online. The potential pitfalls of social media must be seen as an opportunity to lead.

Your digital reputation, and, more importantly, the digital reputation of your students is going to be a major determining factor in that child's future.

We live in a new world with new rules and an expectation of transparency. Your students will be Googled before they get their first interview. Qualman says that 70 percent of job recruiters in the US report they have rejected candidates because of information online.

Have you ever Googled yourself? You should. To keep an eye on your digital footprint, you should Google yourself regularly to see what's out there. Every time I do this exercise in a workshop, participants discover something they didn't know had been shared or posted about them. The only way to protect your digital reputation is to know where you currently stand. If you have a really common name, this could prove more difficult, but you can jump into advanced searches to dig deeper.

One way to keep an eye on your digital reputation is to set up Google Alerts (alerts. google.com) for your name, school, website or blog name. Google Alerts will send you an email notification when something new has been posted about your chosen topic, keywords, or name. I have alerts for my name, Kasey Bell, and for my blog, *Shake Up Learning*. There are a few other people out there with the same name, spelled the same way. So there are a few things I receive that do not have anything to do with me, but I have been able to keep an eye on things posted about me online. I have also received alerts when others have copied my content or presentations and posted them as their own. Setting up Google

Alerts is a great tool for secondary students. Make it a habit to Google yourself on a regular basis to inspect your digital footprint, and teach your students to do the same.

Instant communication allows us to seamlessly connect from just about any corner of the world. The Internet is simply a tool. The power of connections is all about relationships and people. If you want to create a movement and make a difference in the world of education, all you need is the desire to do it.

Every event these days has its own hashtag—conferences, parties, church, brands, even babies! Everyone, everything has a hashtag (cough, cough . . . #ShakeUpLearning). Something as simple as a fourteen-year-old's birthday party has now become a social media event. A couple years ago, my sister asked me to help with my niece's fourteenth birthday party. At first I thought she wanted me to put on my teacher hat and help chaperone. That would have been the typical role for this former middle school teacher, but this was completely different. My sister wanted to tap into my social media and technology skills. I was tasked with not only being the official photographer but the official Instagrammer or what I like to call "Social Media Strategist" for my niece's party. This was a role I had never expected to play. Just five or six years ago, I wouldn't have even understood this concept. Today, a social media strategist is a legit, high-paying job for any company that is paying attention. Are you ready to accept the new roles that are coming your way?

The world is being recorded. Even if you do not post the live video feed of teacher karaoke night, someone else will. Our new and transparent world means the world is watching and recording every move you make.

It used to mean something to see your name in print. Now you can put your name anywhere. This reminds me of one of my favorite movies, *The Jerk*, starring the hilarious Steve Martin as Navin R. Johnson. Navin shouts with excitement, "The new phonebooks are here! The new phonebooks are here!" Keep in mind this was the late seventies, and Navin had led a sheltered life. To see his name in print was so motivating that he proclaimed, "I'm somebody!" Well the medium may have changed, but the power of feeling part of society hasn't. Our students have a need to feel like they are part of the world just like Navin.

Everyone's a marketer. Everyone's a broadcaster. Everyone is a leader or can be. Individuals have more power than ever. You have more power and influence than ever. The explosion of digital tools to share your life, your school, your brand, and broadcast it to the world has shifted decision making across the globe. This means you have the power to make a difference!

As social media continues to evolve and grow more powerful, consider the type of presence you want to model for your students. Educators should maintain a positive social media presence as much as possible. Don't get me wrong—social media is a powerful way to get the attention of someone or some company that has wronged you, but resist the temptation to go on a rant. You don't want to be seen as someone who always throws a hissy fit when things don't go your way. You never know who is watching.

I believe teaching is a calling and that you are a teacher every minute of every day. To think a student won't see that crazy picture you posted on Facebook from your friend's bachelor party is naive. And to think anything you post online is private is completely ignorant. Consider every word, photo, or video you post online as public and permanent. The rules we give students for online behaviors also apply to us as educators. The THINK acronym is a great way to help students (and adults) to consider their content before posting online. THINK before you post. Is it True? Is it Harmful? Is it Illegal? Is it Necessary? Is it Kind?

We must step up as educational leaders and model a positive online presence. This doesn't mean everyone needs hundreds of thousands of followers on Instagram; it just means the good stuff can be found when a student is Googled. Potential employers and college recruiters are not looking for a mystery to solve. They want to know students are real and see what they have accomplished. Participation in the social web should always be positive and a reflection of the student's best self.

Cultivate a Personal Learning Network

Do you have a Personal Learning Network? You should! A personal learning network or PLN is a group of people—other teachers, professionals, leaders—you have connected with or follow online in some way. Moving beyond the "family and friends" connections that most use, consider the importance of learning from your colleagues and peers across the globe. The

Internet has flattened our world and allows us to access other educators and experts at the drop of a hat. Cultivating your own PLN, based on your own needs, interests, grade level, subject area, and passions, is a game changer. Take the time to build your PLN on your favorite platforms, then venture out to newer ones to test the waters. Remember not to immediately dismiss a tool because you don't see how it can be used for your own learning or that of your students. Even applications like Snapchat can be used for good and not evil. Twitter, in particular, has attracted millions of educators across the globe. For me, Twitter has been a greater learning experience than any conference I have ever attended!

When balancing your personal and professional online personas, I believe in avoiding multiple personalities. I recommend you only have one account for the digital networks you use, but you can use them for whatever purposes you need. If you use your Facebook account with family, friends, and colleagues, keep in mind that every post and comment reflects on you as a teacher. If you don't want to connect with your colleagues on Facebook, don't. You have a choice to control whom you connect with and where you connect. Make those choices wisely. If you choose to share personal opinions on Twitter or anywhere else online, treat it as if your grandmother and your boss will read it. Remember, teachers are held to a higher standard, and they should be. Keep in mind that private accounts are rarely completely private, and they are barriers to collaboration and transparency as a learner and leader.

It's imperative to steer clear of absolutes about any digital tool, especially social tools.

When Facebook first became popular, most educators, including myself, said there was no reason students and teachers would need access at school. That belief has changed in a lot of places. Facebook and other digital and social tools have been used to improve communication and collaboration of students, parents, the community, and professionals worldwide. In fact, Facebook and other social networks are now designing specific tools to help you communicate and collaborate on the job. Be cautious, but be open to the possibilities these tools can bring to your classroom and your own learning.

Build a network of educators online using the social media tools of your choice. Twitter happens to be a very popular place for educators to gather, chat, share, and learn. But also find and connect on other social media platforms that meet your needs and interests: Facebook Groups, Google+ Communities, Pinterest, Instagram, SnapChat, blogs, podcasts, YouTube channels, or whatever else tickles your fancy. You don't have to use them all. Just find what works for you, and be sure to join the ever-growing Shake Up Learning Facebook Group at shakeup.link/community. We are always chatting!

Find Your Tribe

Do you have a tribe? Seth Godin defines a tribe as a group of people connected to one another, connected to a leader, and connected to an idea. According to Godin, a group needs only two things to become a tribe: a shared interest and a way to communicate. Tribes are a powerful way to connect, learn, and make a difference in the twenty-first century. But tribes need leaders, and those leaders need tribes.

Most people, including most teachers and students, learn better in small groups. Connecting to learn is a powerful tool to use in the classroom and model for your students. Whether it's online, through social networks, or even going old school face-to-face, you and your students can build a tribe around shared interests and goals.

Connecting with people once depended on geography. Belonging to certain groups, tribes, and networks required you lived in close proximity to other members so you could communicate in person. The Internet has changed all that. Now people can form worldwide movements from wherever they are. Such reach simply wasn't possible twenty-five or thirty years ago. Don't let this opportunity go to waste! We have ways to instantly communicate with just about anyone in the world. Use this access for your own personal learning, and, most of all, for the betterment of your students.

Is your classroom a tribe? Consider the ways your classroom is a tribe or could become a tribe of learners connected to one another, to you as the teacher, and to the bigger ideas and topics in your classroom. Cultivate this community as a tribe. Be open to student feedback, suggestions, and ideas that can contribute to the class and the larger community. Lead your tribe with a focus on building relationships, cultivating curiosity, and supporting student-centered learning goals.

I and my friend Matt Miller, blogger and author of *Ditch That Textbook*, have created a tribe. We built *The Google Teacher Tribe* podcast based on the shared interest of Google-using educators, and we have given them multiple ways to communicate and connect. Members of the tribe can share questions, ideas, and feedback on our blog (GoogleTeacherTribe.com) which includes a tool that allows users to leave a voice message we often play on the podcast. We have a hashtag, #gttribe, that allows the tribe to connect and share via Twitter and other social media platforms. Members of the tribe can also connect with us using the blog, Twitter, or Facebook, and sometimes even in person.

The Google Teacher Tribe has become a way for us to not only share Google tips and ideas for educators, but to create a community that lives, learns, and grows with one another. It's not about Matt and me, it's about the tribe! We are better together. I want to encourage you to engage in groups to connect and learn. Find your tribe, support each other, and connect to something bigger!

Online Resources for Chapter 10

Here you will find resources mentioned in Chapter 10, supplemental resources, videos, as well as new and updated resources.

ShakeUpLearningBook.com/10

Discussion Questions

- How do you use or not use social media? Are you modeling a positive social media presence for your students?
- Do you know a story about a student or an adult who posted something online that cost them dearly?
- Research the power of a hashtag. Go to Twitter.com (even without an account) and search for #edchat or #edtech to see what's being shared and discussed.

Chapter 10 Actions

- Find out the social media policies for your school or district and READ THEM!
- Watch the video from Erik Qualman, "Socialnomics 2017," and reflect on the staggering statistics (shakeup.link/youtuecce).
- Create a PLN of people and organizations: blogs, Twitter, G+, Voxer, Pinterest. Find what works for you. (Learn how and why with this short and sweet video from Common Sense Media: shakeup.link/youtu7d85.)
- Search this database of hashtags and chats to find the area that interests you: shakeup.link/hashtag. (And add your own hashtags and chats to the database by using the form on the page!)
- Participate in a Twitter chat. There are hundreds to choose from! Check the database for topics and times (shakeup.link/hashtag).
- Join #EduMatch to connect with like-minded educators (www.edumatch.org).
- Create your own hashtag for your class or your school.
- Google yourself regularly (and have students Google themselves).
- Set up Google Alerts to monitor a topic of interest (www.google.com/alerts).
- Join the Shake Up Learning Facebook Group (shakeup.link/community).

Connect and Share

Reflection Space

_____

_____

_____

_____

_____

_____

_____

_____

_____

_____

_____

_____

_____

Notes

Qualman, Erik, *What Happens in Vegas Stays on YouTube*, (Cambridge, MA: Equalman Studios, 2014).

Chapter 11

Share Your Voice, and Share Your Story

And do not forget to do good and share with others.
—Hebrews 13:16

Now that we've explored ways to connect and curate, let's talk about what to share. The power of sharing your own unique voice and perspective cannot be oversold. I also believe it's the key to opening the doors to Dynamic Learning Experiences and growth as an educator. We live in a world where people broadcast everything about themselves, perhaps too much. But an educator's voice, thoughts, ideas, reflections, and experiences are valuable and should be shared with others. You don't have to start with anything major or profound—just be open to it. When we reach the last section of this book, I will ask you to share. As I mentioned in the preface, sharing my voice changed everything for me, and I hope it has had an impact on you and your classroom.

Deciding to share doesn't mean you are claiming to be an expert on a particular subject. I'm not sure how many people can claim to be an absolute expert in any one area anymore. The information at our fingertips is growing and everchanging. The day you proclaim to be an expert in Google Docs is the day they release an update! I tread very carefully with

the word expert, but I know how to connect, learn, and teach myself new skills. My blog is a reflection of my own learning and personality. I think the best stories come from learners, not writers. The transparency of learning and failing forward together as a community of educators is much more valuable than advice from so-called experts.

The moment you begin sharing original thoughts, ideas, and content online, you have become a servant leader to the education world. As soon as you start sharing online, you have opened yourself up to questions from the educational community. Sometimes I am still shocked at how many questions I get from teachers across the world, but I try to answer everyone. That's part of my calling as a teacher. If I am at all able, I promise to help you in any way I can. Be prepared. People will question you, but don't let that hold you back. The educational community is very supportive, collaborative, and kind.

Are you still hanging back, lurking on the sidelines? I was just like that, and I challenge you to ask yourself why you're hesitating. Why are you afraid? What is it that you're risking? Be honest in your answers, and consider what you can do to push yourself—and your students—further outside your comfort zone when it comes to connecting online.

Although I believe there is value in blogging for educators at any level, even just as a reflective tool, blogging might not be your calling. So find what does work for you. What are your God-given talents? What is your passion? Be yourself, and let your personality shine through everything you do. For some, this might mean becoming more active in sharing on social media. For others, it might mean launching a blog, a YouTube channel, or a podcast. Just put yourself out there. Share and model this for your students in a positive way. Show them how to share their own unique gifts, ideas, and perspectives in a respectful way.

We live in a connected world where anyone's voice can be heard, and the more we model connecting, curating, and sharing our own unique passions for our students, the more likely they are to take a risk and share their own voices. Every voice matters! Don't be afraid of failure or let your need for perfection paralyze your contribution to the world.

Online Resources for Chapter 11

Here you will find resources mentioned in Chapter 11, supplemental resources, videos, as well as new and updated resources.

ShakeUpLearningBook.com/11

Discussion Questions

- What is it about which you are truly passionate? What gets you fired up?
- How do you share your passions with your students or with the world?
- What are your gifts and talents? How do you share your gifts with others?

Chapter 11 Actions

- Take a tiny plunge, and share something on social media about which you are truly passionate. Use the #ShakeUpLearning hashtag.
- Share why you want to shake up learning in this Flipgrid: flipgrid.com/5e863d.
- Take a giant plunge, and share your voice by starting a place of your own like a blog, podcast, YouTube video, book, or whatever medium tickles your fancy!
- Take the Shake Up Learning Share Your Voice Challenge (shakeup.link/thesh0273)

Share Your Voice, and Share Your Story

Reflection Space

_____

_____

_____

_____

_____

_____

_____

_____

_____

_____

_____

_____

_____

_____

Chapter 12
Go Global

The Internet is becoming the town square
for the global village of tomorrow.
—Bill Gates

Part of creating your dynamic classroom should be going global! Bring the world to your students, and bring your students to the world. It's also our job as teachers to give students a global audience. It is so easy now to allow students to publish their work online for the world. It's amazing how much this will change the quality of what they publish. As soon as they get their first comment, a shift happens.

Publishing for Authentic Audiences

When I taught middle school writing, I would have my kids write for different audiences, but they all knew I was the one who would be reading and assessing their work. I can hear them now: "Why am I writing to an audience of NASA experts? Miss Bell, aren't you the one reading it?" They never took the idea of the audience seriously until I gave them an authentic audience. The moment I allowed them to publish online, it added new value to their work. All students should be publishing their work online—and not only writing assignments but everything, and at every grade level!

Protecting Students vs. Depriving Students

The opportunities for students to publish their work online are almost endless. I still can't believe how many school districts do not allow students to share, communicate, collaborate, and share their learning online. Not too long ago, a senior English teacher contacted me about blogging in the classroom but needed a platform recommendation that could only be accessed by students and teachers inside the district. What's the big secret? Do we really need to hide the learning from the outside world? Seriously, seniors who aren't allowed to share beyond their school? This is ludicrous! This is depriving students of authentic learning experiences they need to be a part of the twenty-first-century workforce.

Please, do not misunderstand me. I believe protecting students is of the utmost importance, but depriving students of critical learning experiences in the process should not be the cost. Why limit the experience of our students by limiting their audience? If all they are exposed to is the opinions, comments, and feedback from their teacher and maybe their parents, they will never truly understand the twenty-first-century idea of sharing. Let the learning light shine! Don't hide it under a bushel. There are many resources that allow students to go global without any unnecessary risks to privacy and safety. We do not have to publish last names, or even first names. In fact, teaching students how to publish and share online without sharing personal information is a future-ready skill. If we keep blocking everything, our students will never gain the skills they need to navigate this ever-changing world.

Publishing for the world can take many forms, and it's important to make sure your students are publishing for an intentional global audience. Sure, a Google Doc can be made public, but because it is public or has a link doesn't mean people will find it, and it definitely doesn't guarantee the intended audience will find it. The intended audience should not have to search to find a student's work. In addition to being intentional about where and how to publish, we must also give the audience a way to comment, provide feedback, and interact with students in some way. Whatever the content, the goal should be to publish with purpose. You could use a blog to allow students to publish lots of different types of content, allow for comments, and share that link with the audience.

Podcasting can also be a powerful publishing tool. Several years ago my students created and produced "Ms. Bell's Chime Time." I had a writing competition among my eighth-grade language arts students and selected the top pieces that would be read on our audio podcast.

That year I happened to have a lot of band and choir students who also competed to create the introductory jingle. There were so many unexpected creations that came out of this project! Then, we published our podcast on iTunes and the students felt like their work had suddenly become highly important. They were excited to share with the world, to get feedback, and to say they were on a podcast. It was a powerful experience for the students, and it opened my eyes as a teacher.

Find the right audience for your students, or help them connect with an authentic audience. This may mean reaching out to authors, experts, and other educators on social media. Tag an organization in your post, join a community, or even email. There is a lot of support for education out there, we just need to ask.

The hashtag #comments4Kids or #kidtweet is a great way to share with like-minded educators on Twitter who could offer feedback or share with their own students. Publishing student videos to YouTube, including a good description and tags, will help students' work be seen and discovered by audiences. Or maybe use a blog or website creator like Blogger, WordPress, Google Sites, Weebly, or Wix to have students share their work, even create online portfolios to showcase work throughout the year. And don't forget the power of audio and simply sharing students' voices. You can easily record audio using tools like GarageBand or Audacity.

I wish there was a magic location to find your audience. Maybe there will be someday, but that too, could be limiting. The idea is get sharing and help your students get some feedback and comments that could help them see not only the power of sharing their work, but also gain powerful insight from someone outside their inner circle.

Every student should have the opportunity to publish for a global audience on a regular basis. Find ways to flatten the walls of your classroom, and allow students to publish their writing, videos, art projects, and even a full e-portfolio online. Instead of telling students to turn in work, we should be telling them to publish it! This will change the quality of their work and help them build a positive online presence.

> Instead of telling students to turn in work, we should be telling them to publish it!

Global Collaboration

Not only should students be publishing their work for the world, they should be globally collaborating as well. I just got off a Google Hangout with a teacher in Australia! It's so simple to bring the power of global collaboration into the classroom. With more international jobs that allow people to work from anywhere in the world, why shouldn't we tap into experts and classrooms in other countries? Why not bring NASA astronauts into a kindergarten classroom in Kalamazoo? Why not connect with another classroom on another continent? Just a few years ago, this meant you had to have expensive video conferencing equipment. Today you just need a good Internet connection, a webcam, and a Google or Skype account to connect with

your favorite authors, experts, and inspirational leaders! This is so much more engaging and powerful than reading about it.

Did you know there are resources solely dedicated to helping teachers and classrooms connect with one another, experts, and other engaging organizations? The Google+ Community, Google Connected Classrooms, is a great place to find ways to bring the world into your classroom. Here you can find out about opportunities for your classroom, subject area, and grade level. You can also propose your own ideas and invite other classes to join you. In addition, Skype has an online community, Skype in the Classroom, where you can connect with like-minded Skype educators. Flipgrid has also developed a global education program call Global Grid Connections where you can connect your classroom with classrooms across the world. Explore connections by grid, age, or subject.

I've seen classes connect with organizations such as Time for Kids, which allowed students to meet Lois Lowry, the author of numerous young adult novels including *The Giver* and *Number the Stars*! I've also seen virtual tours of museums, aquariums, and other places that are sometimes out of our reach. Students get to interact, ask questions, and learn about interesting topics and cultures. Another cool way to use Google Hangouts or Skype is to host a Mystery Hangout or a Mystery Skype through which students play a global guessing game with another classroom somewhere in the world. The aim of the game is to guess the location of the other classroom by asking each other questions.

The possibilities are endless! Consider the ways you can bring the world to your students, and give it a try. If you could invite anyone to your classroom, who would it be? Do it! There is no age limit or subject area restriction to the applications of going global in the classroom and beyond.

Online Resources for Chapter 12

Here you will find resources mentioned in Chapter 12, supplemental resources, videos, as well as new and updated resources.

ShakeUpLearningBook.com/12

Discussion Questions

- In what ways have you helped your students to connect with the world?
- Brainstorm some ideas for your classroom and your students. Where are their opportunities to go global? What work could be published for an intentional and authentic audience?
- Whom would you like to invite into your classroom—maybe an author, an expert, or students from another country?

Chapter 12 Actions

- Join Google Connected Classrooms to connect with other educators, organizations, and classroom projects that bring the field trips to you (shakeup.link/conne4623).
- Share student work on Twitter using the #Comments4Kids or #kidtweet hashtags to get feedback for your students.
- Create a class blog or individual student blogs to allow students to share their learning, projects, and reflections. Encourage students to share links to help them get feedback from an authentic audience.
- Follow the hashtag #GlobalEd for more ideas on ways to go global!

Reflection Space

Chapter 13

Empower Your Students

Who owns the learning?
—Alan November

Students are capable of many great things before they ever leave our classrooms. If we just give them room to make mistakes and experience authentic learning, there is no limit to what they might create. We need to empower our students to have moments of greatness!

One of my favorite YouTube videos is a moment of greatness for fifteen-year-old Jack Andraka as he wins the top Intel award for his creation of a new, non-invasive method of detecting early-stage pancreatic cancer. Every teacher should see this video. Not only is the accomplishment astounding for a fifteen-year-old, his reaction to the award and his joy in winning are priceless. And there are stories about students creating innovative apps, programs, and other products every day.

Another favorite story of mine is about a twelve-year-old app developer, Alex Knoll, who appeared on *The Ellen DeGeneres Show*. Alex started developing Ability App, an application designed to help the disabled navigate public spaces and find safe and reliable services. Alex himself is not disabled, and none of his family members are disabled. But one day he noticed someone in a wheelchair struggling to open a manual door and wondered if there was an app for that. He did some research and didn't find anything that could address this problem, so he decided to create it. How amazing is that? This was a kid who saw a problem and knew he could help develop a solution! Just think of all the skills Alex has cultivated along the way. Not just the technical skills, but the communication—this kid is so articulated—collaboration, research, and the grit it took to make his app happen.

We currently reside in what is often referred to as the industrial revolution model of education, where most learning comes in a one-size-fits-all model, and learning is dictated by age and standardized testing. The factory model doesn't work anymore. Factories don't excite people or motivate change, and the factory model definitely doesn't empower students.

The rest of the world, outside of education, has become personalized. We now have ways to get just about anything customized and personalized. You want your name on a Coke can? It can happen. You want to customize your own perfume? You got it. We no longer have to buy things "off the shelf" or "off the rack." In a world so driven by personalization that values the individual, why are we still giving students a one-size-fits-all education?

What if learning could be customized as easily as a music playlist? It can. We can create custom learning "playlists" that reflect students' needs and interests and make their learning not only a student-centered experience but a student-driven experience. Every child deserves this. It will not happen overnight, but with small steps and pushes in the right direction, we can empower the students in our classrooms. Let's discuss some ways to make that happen.

Empower Students with Voice and Choice

Giving students voice and choice is a vital component to establishing student ownership of learning. You will be pleasantly surprised at the outcome and the depth of understanding when you give them a little extra room to make more decisions on their own. It might be as simple as letting students choose their own reading material, topic, or problem to solve, or it could mean incorporating a genius hour into your curriculum. The following are a few more methods of expanding student voice and choice.

Students Choose Their Own Digital Tools

You can begin by simply providing some choice in how assignments are completed and give students the option to choose their own digital tool. Provide your students with a list of approved digital tools, and allow them to choose the tools they want to use to complete their assignments. Start small, especially if you have never given this option before. I would only give them three to five choices the first time. These should all be tools they have used before and are part of their digital toolbox. Some students will struggle and want you to tell them the correct tool to choose, but this is part of the learning process. Students should learn how to choose the right tool for the job. If you want to go a step further, allow students to propose a digital tool that's not on the list but which would still be subject to your approval. Students have lots of great ideas and tools you've probably never heard of on their devices.

Students Choose Their Own Devices

Some schools have many choices when it comes to devices. Students can bring their own technology, and the school or classroom might have desktops, laptops, iPads, or Chromebooks. If you have this luxury, take advantage of it. Not all devices are equal. I've learned this the hard way. When using their cell phones, it might be easy for students to work in Google Docs or record and edit a video but much more difficult to navigate Google Drawings. Students need to learn the subtleties and limitations of different devices so, when faced with a problem, they can solve it on their own.

Students Choose Their Own Learning Goals

No matter what you call them—student objectives, learning targets, goals—we must help students understand what they are working toward and how to recognize their own progress.

Empower Your Students

That means encouraging students to push themselves beyond the standards required for their subject area and grade level to set goals based on their own interests and passions. Google has many tools that can help with setting and tracking goals. One of my favorites is Google Keep (keep.google.com), which lets teachers and students create a list of learning goals. Students can then refer to these throughout the unit, confer with their teacher to ensure they reach them, and celebrate success! Bonus idea: Add badges and images to Google Keep to gamify the process. Students can also set their own goals, add reminders, and track progress with notes and reflection along the way.

Students Choose Their Own Reading/Topic/Project/Problem

While there are certain topics and skills we must cover in our curriculum, there is also room to give students some choice in the materials. Students could choose from different reading materials or methods for learning content. When it comes to research and other projects, giving students choice of topic or problem can also help them tap into their own interests and reach beyond the regular curriculum.

Give Students Choice with Learning Menus

Learning menus (aka choice boards) are a form of differentiated learning that give students a menu or choice of learning activities. Learning menus and choice boards can be created in a variety of styles and mediums. They've been around for a long time and originated in a static,

paper format. But with digital tools, we can bring the menus to life with interactivity and creation. Menus can be a simple list, a tic-tac-toe- or bingo-style game, or can get as creative and intricate as you like.

For me, learning menus proved an effective way to give my students more choice in their assignments while providing a more flexible learning path. Also known as choice boards, they are a form of differentiated learning and can be used at any grade level and subject area.

Learning Menus Can Be Used with Any Age Group

I have found that menus and choice boards tend to be more popular among elementary teachers, but I used them in my middle school classroom, and now I use them in professional learning workshops with adults. Any grade level or age group can use learning menus!

Learning Menus Can Be Used in Any Subject Area

Since learning menus are so flexible, they can easily be created and adapted for just about any subject area. So no excuses! Any teacher who is willing to try can make use of this student-centered strategy.

My favorite is the Tic-Tac-Toe Learning Menu. If you have never tried learning menus before, this is an easy way to dip your toes in the water. FIGURE 13.1 is an example of a Novel Study Tic-Tac-Toe. This example is a summative assessment OF learning, but it could easily be used for formative assessment as well. No matter what subject you teach, learning menus will offer your students several fun, challenging, and creative choices for showing what they have learned throughout all stages of the learning process. Students learn in many different ways, and each path to the learning goal could look different depending on the student. Choice boards allow you to tap into those varied learning styles and interests. They also offer modifications when necessary.

From a lesson design standpoint, you have complete control over the activities to prevent students from taking the easiest route. One way I control this design is by making the middle space non-negotiable. The one activity I want to insure every student completes is in the center square. This may be reading an article, watching a video, or just creating a slide on a collaborative slide deck to share the learning. By forcing students to make the tic-tac-toe using the middle square, I can design so that I know the other two choices will meet certain learning goals. One section might contain exploration activities and the next might be for creation.

In FIGURE 13.2 is another example of a Tic-Tac-Toe I use in professional learning on Google Chrome. When I teach teachers, I have many levels of expertise, and the beauty of Google Chrome is how it can be a customized learning environment. I try to give teachers the opportunity to explore and find the best apps and extensions for what they teach.

This example is one that would be used as part of the learning process as opposed to the summative assessment style of the novel study example. This is assessment FOR learning or formative assessment. Students get the chance to explore and learn on their own, following a somewhat flexible learning path. The digital tools are used for both learning content and skills and creating something to demonstrate their learning.

My examples are very basic. But I wanted to demonstrate how easily this can be adapted for your own grade and subject area. It doesn't have to be fancy. The quality of the task is much more important.

To show you how versatile learning menus can be, I want to share a couple of examples from my colleagues.

FIGURE 13.3 is an example of an interactive learning menu using Google Slides from Tom Spall, an instructional technology specialist in Brenham ISD in Brenham, Texas. Tom took a more literal approach to the menu idea and created something like a restaurant menu of choices for students. Since Tom helps teachers in his district learn how to integrate technology, this menu has a tool focus so that his teachers can adapt it to fit their individual content needs. I think you will see how easily this can be revised to fit the learning targets for your content area and grade level.

And administrators, don't think you are being left out! My friends Amber Teamann, principal of Whitt Elementary in Wylie, Texas, and her collaborator, Melinda Miller, principal of Willard East Elementary in Willard, Missouri, have created this awesome Professional Development BINGO card (FIGURE 13.4) to help teachers try new things and stay connected over the summer break.

FIGURE 13.1

Tic-Tac-Toe Choice Menu: Novel Study (grades 6-12)

Directions:
Start with number 5 and then make two other choices to make your tic-tac-toe.

1 Create a **fictional interview video** with the protagonist, antagonist, or author where you play the character/author and dress the part. Write a complete script in Google Docs and submit with the video.	**2** Create four **character trading cards** using the digital tool of your choice. Remember to include the character's name, an image, and at least five characteristics for each character.	**3** **Write a diary** from the point of view of one of the story's main characters that they would have written before, during, or after the book's events. Remember that the character's thoughts and feelings are very important in a diary.
4 Create an **interactive digital timeline** of events from your book. Include important dates, character introductions, conflicts and resolution, images to represent each event, and links to additional information, videos, etc.	**5** **Write a one-paragraph summary** of your novel, and share on a slide in our **collaborative slide deck [insert your own link]**. Add an image of the book cover and links to your other two projects.	**6** If this novel had a **soundtrack**, what would it be? Create a YouTube playlist with at least 10 songs that would make a great soundtrack. Explain each of your choices in a Google Doc and where they fit in the story arc.
7 Create a **comic strip** retelling the story in your own words. Be sure to include all of the important characters, exciting events, conflicts, and resolution.	**8** Create a video **book trailer** using the digital tool of your choice. Remember to include music to set the tone, and tell a brief story about the central conflict and characters without revealing too much! Tease the audience!	**9** Create a new **book jacket** for the novel. Use the digital tool of your choice or the artistic medium of your choice (draw, paint, etc.). Remember to include a summary about the author and an eye-catching cover image.

Created by Kasey Bell
www.ShakeUpLearning.com

FIGURE 13.2

Tic-Tac-Toe Choice Menu:
Google Chrome PD for Teachers

Directions:

Start with number 5 and then make two other choices to make your tic-tac-toe. Remember to add notes to the Collaborative Notes as you go! Feel free to download apps and extensions you are interested in, and play!

① **Explore** this database of Chrome apps and extensions to find ideas for you and your students. Share two of your favorites in the collaborative notes.	**②** **Explore** and search the Chrome Web Store Education Category for apps and extensions that will support learning in your classroom. Share two of your favorites in the collaborative notes.	**③** **Explore** this vetted list of Chrome apps and teacher reviews from Common Sense Media to find the best for the classroom. Share two of your favorites in the collaborative notes.
④ **Explore** this Google Chrome Pinterest Board to find ideas for you and your students. Share two of your favorites in the collaborative notes.	**⑤** **START HERE!** Watch this video: A Chrome Superhero.	**⑥** Using the Chrome App of your choice, create a **"Meet the Teacher"** introduction. Share a link in the collaborative notes. (Suggestions: Canva, Flipgrid, Powtoon, or Google Slides.)
⑦ Create a **classroom procedures and rules presentation** using the Chrome App of your choice. Share a link in the collaborative notes. (Suggestions: PowToon, Google Slides, Animoto or Canva).	**⑧** Create an **interactive video lesson** for your students using EdPuzzle. Share a link in the collaborative notes.	**⑨** Create a **digital story** about a student who changed your thinking, using the Chrome App of your choice. Share a link in the collaborative notes. (Suggestions: WeVideo, Storybird, Buncee, or Animoto.)

Created by Kasey Bell
www.ShakeUpLearning.com

FIGURE 13.3

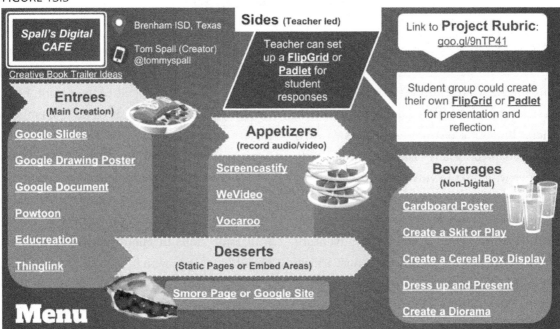

FIGURE 13.4

PD BINGO

Attend An Edcamp	Subscribe to an educational blog	Read 1 PD book & Tweet 1 fun thing	Create an Instagram account.	Revamp your "Back to School" teacher letter.
Tag or send a teacher friend an Instagram post with an activity to try.	Find ONE new app to use in your 1st IFD.	Use Adobe Spark to create an image with a fave quote and share!	Find a FREE TpT resource for Guided Reading and share.	Follow 5 new teachers on Twitter.
Create a NEW 1st Day of School activity and share.	Snapchat...share a selfie with a fun filter!	FREE SPACE	Find someone you feel like you can learn from and plan to visit them in the fall!	Watch an educational "TED Talk."
Find and share a flexible seating management strategy.	Find a FREE TpT resource for Guided Math and share.	Comment on an educational blog post.	Reach out to new teacher. (Invite to lunch/coffee/ write welcome note.)	Tweet, text, or Facebook a selfie doing any of these things!
Send an email to 3 colleagues complimenting them for something they do in their classroom.	Create and/or share an educational Pinterest board.	Participate in a Twitter Chat Retweet 5 Things	Share one professional goal.	Create an "All About Me" poster/anchor chart/activity for 1st week of school

@8AMBER & @MMILLER7571

I think PD BINGO is genius! It's not overly complicated. It's doable. Of course, Amber and Melinda make it extra fun with some giveaways for teachers who get a BINGO. Empower teacher learners! But think of the possibilities . . . this could be adapted for any classroom, even made interactive with links to videos, tutorials, articles, and creation tools.

I urge you to consider other types of learning menus, such as a choose-your-own-adventure setup, bingo cards, or gamified menus. I have a few blog posts on this topic, including free templates so be sure to access the chapter resources on the companion website.

Empower Students with Entrepreneurial Skills

As mentioned earlier in this book, entrepreneurship is on the rise, and it requires a certain skill set. Not only do students need to become risk-takers and problem-solvers, they need to learn leadership skills, be independent learners, and develop a good work ethic.

Building a good work ethic in students is not easy. How do we teach this? It must be modeled, coached, and cultivated, and it can be instilled at home and in school. Teachers and parents should model a good work ethic and a dedication to getting a job done right. Being a part of the grind and owning the work is a skill our students need.

Leadership skills are key to entrepreneurial success, because genuine leadership is not just about management or taking control. Good leaders know how to make the most of the skills of their team, how to carefully listen to the ideas of others, empower others to make decisions, and orchestrate a successful path toward the goal. Sound familiar? Your role as a facilitator of learning is much more of a leadership role than a traditional teacher role. Give students an opportunity to develop leadership skills through role-play and project-based learning, which require them to learn collaboratively and be open to other people's ideas.

We need to give every student the skills needed to survive in our new and ever-changing economy as well as the ability to own and operate their own businesses. I bet many of you have students who are already running their own enterprises! Students can succeed and begin building their own online business today, and many already have. Prepare your students for the jobs of tomorrow and foster an entrepreneurial learning environment in your class this year.

Practice the Art of Curiosity

Curiosity was a driving force for renowned theoretical physicist Albert Einstein. Why can't it be that way for our students? With passion-driven learning experiences, such as 20% Time and Genius Hour, we can help students pursue their interests. When was the last time you were given time by your teacher or employer to explore the things that interest you most? Our youngest students come

Always open the curiosity door.

to us so curious about everything they encounter, asking, "Why?" repeatedly about everything. By the time they reach secondary school, students have been conditioned—or schooled, unfortunately—and are far less curious. They simply want to know the shortest way to the correct answer, which is often found in the back of the book.

In the Netflix series, *Stranger Things*, the central characters are middle-school-aged kids with a curiosity for all things science and technology. One of their teachers, Mr. Clark, guides their passions by encouraging them "to always open the curiosity door." Isn't that a great way to think of it?

How do we bring back that youthful curiosity? We start by giving students opportunities to explore their own interests. Of course, building more authentic learning experiences for our students will also help them understand there is more than one way to solve a problem. As Jaime Casap, Chief Education Evangelist at Google, says, "Don't ask students what they want to be when they grow up; ask them what problems they want to solve."

Empower Independent Learners

We've all heard and discussed the importance of collaboration in the twenty-first century. It is a highly valued skill for many jobs, and it is something that can be crucial to the learning and creation process. But collaboration in the classroom often gets watered down into ineffective group work simply to check a box. While collaborative learning is essential, it can stifle some students. The world tends to reward the extroverted learner who does well in groups while undervaluing the introvert. As an introvert myself, I know forcing some students into groups—or even just making them sit in groups—can be challenging, unfair, and ultimately counterproductive. While collaboration is an important part of entrepreneurship, many business owners do choose to go the solo route. We must continually strive to find the balance between collaboration and independent learning. A good rule is to always balance the learning experiences in your classroom to enhance your students' strengths, build confidence, and set them up for success.

So how do we do this? How do we cultivate these skills in our classrooms without turning into a startup incubator? (That's not a bad idea, actually!) This is something we will discuss in the Dynamic Learning section of the book when we move beyond the subject area and grade level.

Online Resources for Chapter 13

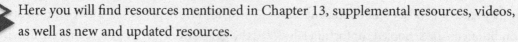

Here you will find resources mentioned in Chapter 13, supplemental resources, videos, as well as new and updated resources.

ShakeUpLearningBook.com/13

Discussion Questions

- In what ways do you empower the students in your classroom?
- How are you encouraging independent learning with your students?
- How do you give students voice and choice in their learning?
- How do you help students practice the art of curiosity?

Chapter 13 Actions

- Brainstorm ways you could increase student choice in your classroom.
- Create a learning experience giving students the digital tool of choice to demonstrate their learning.
- Create a learning menu or choice board of activities for your students. Use my Pinterest board for inspiration: shakeup.link/85bes3299.
- Plan a goal-setting discussion with your students to work on learning goals in and out of the classroom.

Reflection Space

_____

_____

_____

_____

_____

_____

Empower Your Students

_____

_____

_____

_____

_____

_____

_____

_____

_____

_____

_____

Notes

Casap, Jamie, *Twitter*, Jan. 24, 2015, twitter.com/jcasap/status/559048742574522368?lang=en.

Chapter 14
The Dynamic Learning Model

Technology is nothing. What's important is that you have faith
in people, that they're basically good and smart, and if you give
them tools, they'll do wonderful things with them.
—Steve Jobs

love the quote above from Steve Jobs about having faith in people, but I would like to put a twist on it: Have faith in students! Don't underestimate what they can do. Big or small, differently abled or gifted, don't ever hold back because you think something is too challenging for the group you teach. They just might surprise you!

The idea of dynamic learning is something I have explored deeply. I continually seek ways to compile and describe all the ways that technology can take learning to new heights and push boundaries. Traditional teaching must change. It has to. It's simply no longer enough. Why do we still employ so many static assignments and activities that never get the chance to transform learning for our students? We must move past the idea of doing old things with new tools and truly make the most of what this wonderful, twenty-first-century world has to offer.

As I've mentioned, I taught English Language Arts, and one of the lessons I would teach every year was about the difference between static and dynamic characters. As I started trying to

think of ways to describe a different approach to learning, the word dynamic came to mind. According to Google dictionary, dynamic means "characterized by constant change, activity, or progress." The word dynamic fits perfectly, and I don't think any other word in the English language could better express what I am trying to say. We can do so many things that make learning more dynamic by reaching beyond what we thought was possible. We've explored changes in technology, learning, and what it means for the future, and these changes present us with the opportunity to move learning from static to dynamic.

Dynamic Learning Versus Static Learning

Let's begin with some definitions and comparisons to better understand the contrast between static learning and dynamic learning.

Like it or not, I tend to think of static learning as the old way and dynamic learning as the new way. Like those unchanging characters in the novels I once taught, static learning is characterized by an overall lack of movement, growth, and action. It's learning that happens in short bursts and is most often demonstrated by the learner completing one-and-done activities, short-term assignments, and stand-alone worksheets—all confined within the bounds of the traditional school day.

In comparison, dynamic learning is characterized by constant change and activity.

This learning takes place organically, growing and evolving through more unconventional means, with the learner collaborating, creating, and communicating to demonstrate progress and mastery. Dynamic Learning also extends beyond the boundaries of a traditional school day, beyond the physical location of the classroom, beyond using tools as digital substitutes, or even the traditional notion of hard-and-fast due dates.

FIGURE 14.1

DYNAMIC LEARNING

Dynamic learning is characterized by constant change and activity. This learning takes place organically, growing and evolving through more unconventional means, with the learner collaborating, creating, and communicating to demonstrate progress and mastery. Dynamic Learning also extends beyond the boundaries of a traditional school day, beyond the physical location of the classroom, beyond using tools as digital substitutes, or even the traditional notion of hard-and-fast due dates.

STATIC LEARNING

Static learning is characterized by an overall lack of movement, growth, and action. It's learning that happens in short bursts and is most often demonstrated by the learner completing one-and-done activities, short-term assignments, and stand-alone worksheets—all confined within the bounds of the traditional school day.

© 2018 ShakeUpLearning.com

The Dynamic Learning Model

Is the learning in your classroom static or dynamic? Are your students spending time on orderly, one-and-done activities, or are they getting a little messy and exploring and evolving throughout the year? With digital tools such as G Suite for Education, which are available around the clock, learning doesn't have to start and stop when the bell rings. Learning can take on a life of its own. The focus shifts to the process and not just the end product or assessment. This concept alone can change the way we facilitate all learning in the classroom. Be boundless!

Consider the dreaded worksheet. There might be good, critical thinking questions on that worksheet, but once it is turned in, that's the end of that line of thinking. Paper activities make it difficult to allow learning to grow organically and to share or collaborate. You aren't still on MySpace, so why are you still assigning worksheets? Now compare that worksheet with a Google Doc, a blog, or a website. Digital tools like these give us the opportunity to be more dynamic because they can be updated, provide immediate feedback, offer real-time assistance, and connect to global resources. My website (www.ShakeUpLearning.com) would be worthless to me if I couldn't update it and make changes and add additional content. That's what makes the Web so powerful: It's alive and constantly changing.

Now go back to that worksheet and ponder how it could grow into something more dynamic, creative, and meaningful. What if instead of just writing the answers to questions on a piece of paper, students were demonstrating their knowledge through a collaborative Google Drawing of the Battle of the Alamo? What if they could include labels, historical figures, videos, and links and were able to tell the story in a completely new and interactive way? What if, even after their work had been assessed, they were allowed to continue developing the topics that piqued their interest?

Consider a research project on emerging technology. Depending on what day you do the research, that project could look very different. What if this was a project that students continued to add to, learn from, and create throughout the school year? What if we could combine that with their reflections and publish it to the world as a blog? Why not consider activities that allow students to continue to grow and share ideas throughout a unit of study, an entire six- or nine-week period, or even the entire year?

Education, just like any field, is loaded with trends and buzzwords that tend to get thrown around like dough in a New York City pizza parlor. We are constantly trying to find new ways to support our students, and often we are attracted to the next big thing, the next magic acronym that's going to solve all our problems. Teaching isn't that simple. It is much more art than science. Formulas don't work because one size doesn't fit all teachers, and one size doesn't fit all students.

You will see that the concepts presented in this chapter (and in the Dynamic Learning Model) are not new, although they could be new to you. My goal isn't to invent the next new thing or reinvent the wheel. I'm trying to put the wheel back together. My goal is to break down the barriers to progress and shake up learning.

I want to gather up some of the great ideas about transforming teaching and learning and place them into a meaningful framework for teachers—one that makes sense for the novice teacher, the technophobe teacher, the old-school, traditional teacher, or even the innovative teacher—to help them see the bigger picture. Most of us do not work in ideal schools with an overflow of funding and resources, and we don't have time to wait for that to happen. We can't chase every new idea and trend. We can't just keep piloting and never let the transformation work its way into the mainstream K–12 classroom. We must forge ahead and make meaningful changes, wherever we can, in our school districts, campuses, and classrooms. One step at a time.

Dynamic learning is a way to put it all together. There is not just one correct way to do anything. There is not just one trendy, exciting thing to try in the classroom. There are hundreds of new things to do in the classroom: Genius Hour, Maker Education, Project-Based Learning, Problem-Based Learning, Challenge-Based Learning, Robotics, Coding, Gamification, STEM, STEAM, lions and tigers and bears, oh my! There are countless ways to create a culture of innovation, to help students tap into creativity, to help students learn how to do things differently, and to break the bounds of the traditional classroom.

Sadly, we tend to gravitate to the newest fads and end up spending too much time and money chasing trends instead of looking at the bigger picture and investing in incremental changes that could truly make a difference. Many teachers just don't get it, especially teachers who are new to technology integration, or even more experienced teachers who just can't wrap their heads around how to use new strategies and new technologies in the classroom in a meaningful way. We need to avoid fads and focus on substance, and to do that we must unlearn our conventional notions of what learning looks like in the classroom.

To help better illustrate the difference between static and dynamic learning, I have put together a "Do This, Not That" list of learning experiences.

As we begin to dig deeper into what dynamic learning looks like, I want to be clear—it does not hinge on technology or any digital tools. In fact, the word technology is not included in the dynamic learning definition or infographic. That's because technology can be integrated anywhere. Technology doesn't need to be explicit. It needs to be seamlessly infused where it can enhance the learning.

You will never see me publish an infographic of dynamic learning tools. A digital tool is not inherently dynamic. It is the student's use of tools and the ways it's used to create and demonstrate learning that is dynamic. Dynamic learning might include this use of digital tools, or it might not. Technology is not a requirement for dynamic learning, but it can make dynamic learning possible.

The Dynamic Learning Model

As you may have guessed, I'm a fan of infographics and anything visual that can help us process information. I created this learning model first for myself as a way of seeing how

FIGURE 14.2

DYNAMIC LEARNING v. STATIC LEARNING

DYNAMIC LEARNING	STATIC LEARNING
Dynamic learning is characterized by constant change and activity. This learning takes place organically, growing and evolving through more unconventional means, with the learner collaborating, creating, and communicating to demonstrate progress and mastery. Dynamic Learning also extends beyond the boundaries of a traditional school day and beyond the physical location of the classroom.	Static learning is learning that is lacking in movement, action, or change, especially in a way that is not engaging—where learning happens in short bursts and is often demonstrated in one-and-done activities, short-term assignments, or worksheets (even digital worksheets), that are confined within the traditional bounds of the school system, school day, and the school walls.

DO THIS	NOT THAT
Skype interview with a war survivor in another country.	Research "paper" on World War II.
Collaborative and interactive online eBook about the life of Edgar Allan Poe and published to a global audience.	Edgar Allan Poe author study worksheet packet.
A class-created Google Earth Tour project touring the capitals of the United States and shared with classes across the U.S.	Labeling and coloring a paper map of the capitals of the United States.
A public class website on inspiring historical figures (past and present) in which additional content is added throughout the year.	Written biography of Winston Churchill.
Interactive website and blog about a Science Fair project including hypothesis, data, video of experiments, reflection, milestones, conclusion, and a place for comments.	Tri-fold poster display of Science Fair project.
Genius Hour project developing a prototype of a new product that solves a real-world problem.	Worksheet about the scientific method.

For more information: shakeup.link/dothisnotthat

© Shake Up Learning 2018

each component fits together. I am also a big proponent of learning models that help illustrate important ideas. Enter the Dynamic Learning Model.

Take a look at FIGURE 14.3

- At the center of it all (the target, if you will) are our keywords: Dynamic Learning.

- The first inner circle contains the Four Cs:
  o Creativity
  o Communication
  o Collaboration
  o Critical Thinking

- The next circle is full of icons to represent the various ways we can go beyond traditional learning. We will dig into the "beyonds" section in the next chapter, but keep this in mind:
  o BEYOND the Bell
  o BEYOND the Grade Level and Subject Area
  o BEYOND the Walls
  o BEYOND the Tools
  o BEYOND the Due Date

- The outer ring is all about planning and implementation, represented as a cycle, like the learning cycle itself.
  o Purposeful Planning
  o Focused on Learning Outcomes
  o Fearless Implementation
  o Facilitated with Finesse
  o Honest Reflection
  o Share with the World

We will focus on the outer ring in Part Three of this book, Equipping for Impact.

Before we break this down, I want you to take a moment to soak this in and think about how this brings together all the concepts we have explored so far. What do these ideas already mean to you?

FIGURE 14.3

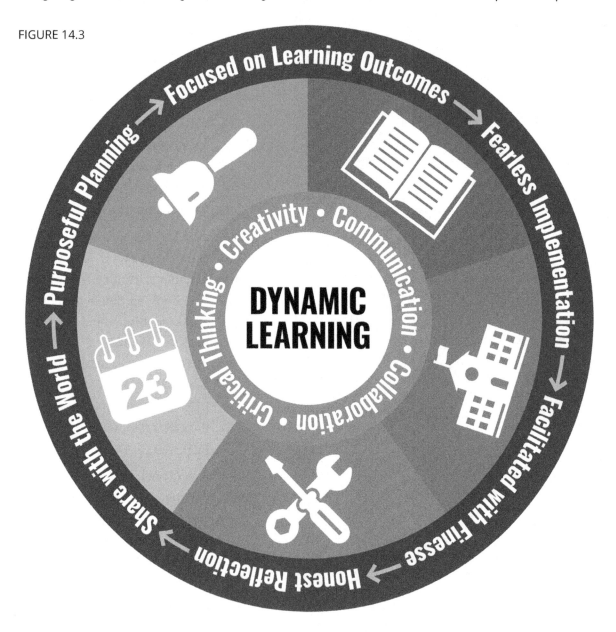

Essential Components for Dynamic Learning

Dynamic learning is not a task that can simply be checked off a list. Just like teaching, it is more of an art form than a science. Even with small tweaks, you will begin to see tiny transformations in your classroom. If you are ready for a bigger leap and want the learning to truly become more dynamic, there are some essential components you will want to incorporate.

The Four Cs: Let's start with the heart of the Dynamic Learning Model, the Four Cs: creativity, communication, collaboration, and critical thinking skills. These skills have been mentioned and sprinkled throughout the entire book. The Four Cs are integral to dynamic learning, and every Dynamic Learning Experience should include at least one of the Four Cs. For our purposes, we will define these skills as the following.

Creativity: The use of imagination and original ideas to solve problems and create. (Examples: Cultivate creativity and innovation with projects that require students to design original solutions, invent something new to solve a problem, or integrate art and design with room to fail.)

Communication: The ability to effectively and clearly communicate for a variety of audiences and using a variety of tools and mediums. (Examples: Give students opportunities to interact with adult experts, authors, and real-world audiences. Let them experience speaking and presenting.)

Collaboration: Learning and working in groups or teams, locally and/or globally, to achieve a goal. (Examples: Ensure there is purpose to the collaboration and not just group work. Form partners and teams strategically with assigned leadership roles, include team-building exercises, establish collaboration guidelines and shared decision-making.)

Critical Thinking: The ability to conceptualize, analyze, synthesize, and evaluate information for the purpose of deeper understanding, problem-solving, and guiding action. (Examples: Create learning experiences, such as mock trials or debates, scientific investigations, interpreting events in history or literature, or design challenges.)

In what ways are you already integrating the Four Cs into your curriculum? Notice again that each of these is not explicitly talking about using technology. It's about active learning and skills for the twenty-first century.

Every Dynamic Learning Experience should integrate one or more of the Four Cs with purpose toward the learning targets. They also work together very seamlessly, and all can be implemented across grade levels and subject areas.

In the next few chapters you will begin to see how all the big ideas will fit within the Four Cs and help you go beyond the conventional classroom.

The ISTE Standards for Students: Another crucial component for dynamic learning is including the ISTE Standards for Students. While these standards are not explicitly part of the Dynamic Learning Model, they align very nicely to the Four Cs but take things to a more specific level and definitely align to the ways we can go beyond old-school assignments.

For the purpose of defining learning goals, we will use these standards to guide our planning. I think you will see how well these standards fit with the ideas presented in this book, but using

FIGURE 14.4

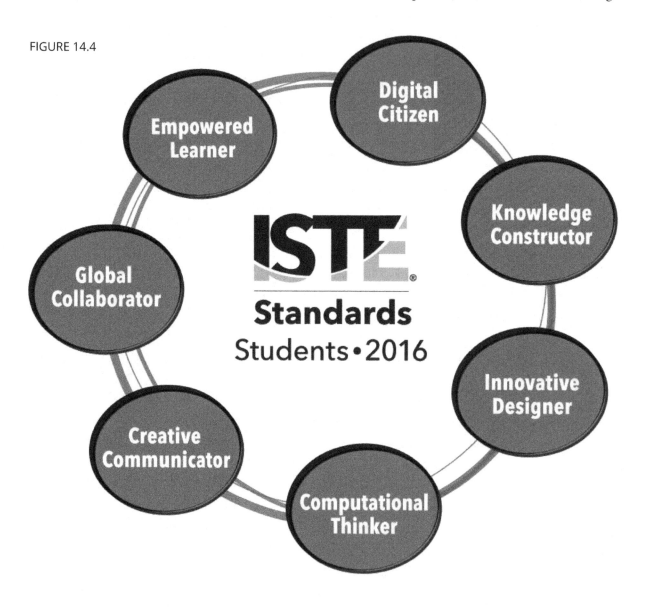

The Dynamic Learning Model

standards as guides for our learning targets will help insure our dynamic learning goals are met. These standards are learner driven and have a clear and present focus on learning, not technology, as well as encouraging exploration and discovery:

1. **Empowered Learner**

   Students leverage technology to take an active role in choosing, achieving, and demonstrating competency in their learning goals, informed by the learning sciences. Students . . .

   a. Articulate and set personal learning goals, develop strategies leveraging technology to achieve them, and reflect on the learning process itself to improve learning outcomes.

   b. Build networks and customize their learning environments in ways that support the learning process.

   c. Use technology to seek feedback that informs and improves their practice and to demonstrate their learning in a variety of ways.

   d. Understand the fundamental concepts of technology operations, demonstrate the ability to choose, use, and troubleshoot current technologies and are able to transfer their knowledge to explore emerging technologies.

2. **Digital Citizen**

   Students recognize the rights, responsibilities, and opportunities of living, learning, and working in an interconnected digital world,

and they act and model in ways that are safe, legal, and ethical. Students . . .

   a. Cultivate and manage their digital identity and reputation and are aware of the permanence of their actions in the digital world.

   b. Engage in positive, safe, legal, and ethical behavior when using technology, including social interactions online or when using networked devices.

   c. Demonstrate an understanding of and respect for the rights and obligations of using and sharing intellectual property.

   d. Manage their personal data to maintain digital privacy and security and are aware of data-collection technology used to track their navigation online.

3. **Knowledge Constructor**

   Students critically curate a variety of resources using digital tools to construct knowledge, produce creative artifacts, and make meaningful learning experiences for themselves and others. Students . . .

   a. Plan and employ effective research strategies to locate information and other resources for their intellectual or creative pursuits.

   b. Evaluate the accuracy, perspective, credibility, and relevance of information, media, data, or other resources.

   c. Curate information from digital resources using a variety of tools and methods to create collections of artifacts that demonstrate meaningful connections or conclusions.

d. Build knowledge by actively exploring real-world issues and problems, developing ideas and theories, and pursuing answers and solutions.

4. Innovative Designer

Students use a variety of technologies within a design process to identify and solve problems by creating new, useful, or imaginative solutions. Students . . .

a. Know and use a deliberate design process for generating ideas, testing theories, creating innovative artifacts, or solving authentic problems.

b. Select and use digital tools to plan and manage a design process that considers design constraints and calculated risks.

c. Develop, test, and refine prototypes as part of a cyclical design process.

d. Exhibit a tolerance for ambiguity, perseverance, and the capacity to work with open-ended problems.

5. Computational Thinker

Students develop and employ strategies for understanding and solving problems in ways that leverage the power of technological methods to develop and test solutions. Students . . .

a. Formulate problem definitions suited for technology-assisted methods such as data analysis, abstract models, and algorithmic thinking in exploring and finding solutions.

b. Collect data or identify relevant data sets, use digital tools to analyze them, and represent data in various ways to facilitate problem-solving and decision-making.

c. Break problems into component parts, extract key information, and develop descriptive models to understand complex systems or facilitate problem-solving.

d. Understand how automation works and use algorithmic thinking to develop a sequence of steps to create and test automated solutions.

6. Creative Communicator

Students communicate clearly and express themselves creatively for a variety of purposes using the platforms, tools, styles, formats, and digital media appropriate to their goals. Students . . .

a. Choose the appropriate platforms and tools for meeting the desired objectives of their creation or communication.

b. Create original works or responsibly repurpose or remix digital resources into new creations.

c. Communicate complex ideas clearly and effectively by creating or using a variety of digital objects such as visualizations, models, or simulations.

d. Publish or present content that customizes the message and medium for their intended audiences.

7. Global Collaborator

Students use digital tools to broaden their perspectives and enrich their learning by collaborating with others and working effectively in teams, locally and globally.

The Dynamic Learning Model

Students . . .

a. Use digital tools to connect with learners from a variety of backgrounds and cultures, engaging with them in ways that broaden mutual understanding and learning.

b. Use collaborative technologies to work with others, including peers, experts, or community members, to examine issues and problems from multiple viewpoints.

c. Contribute constructively to project teams, assuming various roles and responsibilities to work effectively toward a common goal.

d. Explore local and global issues and use collaborative technologies to work with others to investigate solutions.

As you peruse the standards, think about the big picture. These standards are a great way to begin thinking differently about your assignments. When you begin the planning phase, consider these as your dynamic learning targets in conjunction with your content area standards. Where do you already see this type of learning happening? Where would it naturally fit in your curriculum?

Dynamic Learning Upgrades

I bet you have some amazing lessons in your bag of tricks that just need an upgrade. Sometimes you can make a lesson more dynamic simply by giving students some choice or allowing them to publish for an intentional global audience. Remember, dynamic learning is not about having technology in your lesson. It's about bringing learning to life and letting it grow and evolve in new ways.

Don't misunderstand me. We all still must operate within the confines of our school systems, but I believe we can meaningfully incorporate more dynamic learning strategies in our classrooms without ignoring the many boxes we have to check. And I don't think it is a choice anymore. We are doing students a disservice if we aren't moving beyond traditional learning with the technology we now have within our grasp. Just small pushes against the walls can bring about meaningful change,

one

  small

    step

      at

        a

          time.

That's all it takes. I'm not asking teachers to immerse their classrooms in these ideas overnight. I'm just asking educators to consider the transformation that is possible and try some new things. Even in small increments, we can make a big difference and better prepare our students for the future.

Online Resources for Chapter 14

Here you will find resources mentioned in Chapter 14, supplemental resources, videos, as well as new and updated resources.

ShakeUpLearningBook.com/14

Discussion Questions

- What are the barriers and challenges you face when you try to integrate the Four Cs and the ISTE Standards for students?
- What are some dynamic learning upgrades you could use in your favorite learning experiences?
- What is one thing you could try next week?

Chapter 14 Actions

- Dig deeper into the ISTE Standards for students at shakeup.link/istes, and see how they can be applied in your grade level and subject area.
- Look at your curriculum and lesson plans, and make a list of five places where you see opportunities for dynamic learning. Share that list with a fellow teacher and trade some ideas.
- To learn more about the Four Cs, go to shakeup.link/p21 and shakeup.link/neaguide. Then make a list of three to five ways you can integrate the Four Cs in your classroom.

Reflection Space

_____

_____

_____

_____

_____

_____

The Dynamic Learning Model

Chapter 15
The Dynamic Learning Framework

To move from something that is a noun to something
dynamic and unpredictable, to something living and
present tense, is to move from law to grace.
—William P. Young, *The Shack*

The Dynamic Learning Model is at the center of what I like to refer to as the Dynamic Learning Framework, which focuses on the Dynamic Learning Characteristics, ways to go beyond static, one-and-done activities. In this chapter we will take a closer look at the framework (pictured in FIGURE 15.1) and break down each section.

Dynamic Learning Characteristics
Beyond the Bell (a Mindset)

Learning doesn't have to end when the bell rings. With digital tools and devices that are available twenty-four hours a day and seven days a week, students can continue to learn, collaborate, grow, and dig deeper into their learning on their own terms. And by extending learning beyond the school day, I don't mean homework. This is a mindset that's based on a belief that learning can take place anytime and anywhere. This doesn't mean simply working after school. Homework and working past the bell is not what this is all about. It is a continuous learning mindset.

To become dynamic learners, students must take ownership of not only their learning but their time. They must resolve to move beyond the Game of School and realize they have the power to connect to other resources to teach themselves new concepts and skills. They must take responsibility for learning how to solve their own problems.

Strategies to Move Beyond the Bell

Talk it Out: Start a discussion with students about their learning. What do they like? What do they struggle with? What would they learn if they had complete control over time and place? Remember, this is more a mindset than a specific skill.

Learning Goals: Help students write their own learning goals—goals aligned with what they are learning in class but also extending to their own interests and passions. Help them develop a continuous learning mindset. What problems would they like to solve? What's a skill or concept they've always wanted to learn?

FIGURE 15.1

DYNAMIC LEARNING

Use these strategies to go BEYOND traditional learning and make it more DYNAMIC!

BEYOND THE BELL

Learning doesn't have to end when the bell rings. With digital tools and devices that are available 24/7, students can continue to learn, collaborate, grow, and dig deeper into their learning on their own terms. This doesn't mean homework. This is a mindset for students that means learning can take place anytime, anywhere, and students can own it.

BEYOND THE GRADE LEVEL & SUBJECT

Let's take kids off the conveyor belt of education and give them opportunities to learn about the things that interest them beyond the subject areas we teach and even beyond what it says they should learn in each grade level. Learning doesn't have to fit inside a box.

BEYOND THE DUE DATE

Consider allowing students to continue the work that interests them beyond the final assessment of the assignment or task. Thinking, learning, and exploring, shouldn't be stifled simply because it was time to turn it in.

Circle diagram center: **DYNAMIC LEARNING**

Inner ring: Creativity • Communication • Collaboration • Critical Thinking

Outer ring: Purposeful Planning → Focused on Learning Outcomes → Fearless Implementation → Facilitated with Finesse → Honest Reflection ← Share with the World

BEYOND THE WALLS

Bring the world to your students, and bring your students to the world! Every student in every grade should have opportunities to connect and learn globally as well as publish their work for a global and intentional audience.

BEYOND THE TOOLS

Think beyond using digital tools to do traditional things like typing a paper. Use digital tools to do NEW things! Just going paperless or digital isn't enough; use tools to go further, go deeper and extend the learning, and consider using tools in alternative ways—beyond their original purpose.

Created by:

© 2018 ShakeUpLearning.com

The Dynamic Learning Framework

Try This: "Student-Created Vision Boards with Google Slides"

What Is a Vision Board?

A vision board is a collection of images and words that represent the things you want in life—the things you want to do, the things you want to learn, the things you want to be. I create a vision board for myself each year, and I got to thinking about how valuable this experience could be for our students.

Often, vision boards are not digital; they are hands-on creations, with images cut from magazines, glued together on posterboard. While this is fun and tangible, it may not be as classroom friendly.

The Digital Vision Board

You can create digital versions of vision boards using the tools of your choice. Google Slides or Google Drawings stand out as obvious choices when it comes to G Suite. I created the student example in FIGURE 15.2 using Google Slides and the Unsplash photos add-on to show how easy this activity can be. Of course, a digital version allows you to carry it with you wherever you go and regularly reflect on your progress.

FIGURE 15.2

Try This: Tracking Student-Created Learning Goals in Google Keep

Google Keep offers a wonderful way to track to-do lists, notes, and more. It's a great fit for tracking learning goals. Students can create a new note with their own learning goals as well as those the teacher may share. They can also be collaborative so the student can share with you, the teacher. Together you can track the student's progress (see FIGURE 15.3).

FIGURE 15.3

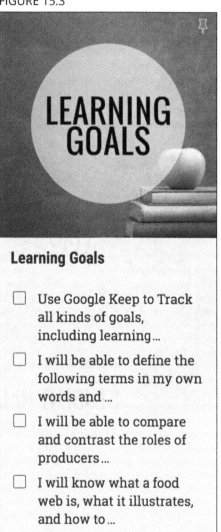

Beyond the Grade Level and Subject Area

As Sir Ken Robinson tells us in his TED Talk on creativity in education, the education system we have today is still based on a factory model in which students are basically placed on a conveyor belt. What they learn is what fits inside the factory "box," all dictated by their ages and grade levels. Why can't we work within the confines of the system to allow students to pursue their own interests and give them more voice and choice? Can't we allow teachers to collaborate to create more interdisciplinary activities and projects? Let's take kids off the conveyor belt of education and give them opportunities to explore the world and move beyond the subject areas we teach. Learning doesn't have to fit inside a box.

Strategies to Move Beyond the Grade Level or Subject Area

Design Thinking: Design Thinking is a problem-solving process to help us redefine problems and challenge assumptions in an attempt to identify alternative strategies and solutions. As stated in *Launch*, "It's more of a way of solving problems that encourages positive risk-taking and creativity."

Design Thinking has four phases: (1) gather inspiration, (2) generate ideas, (3) make ideas tangible, and (4) share your story. This process can be used in Genius Hour, Maker Projects, and other types of project-based learning activities. Using this protocol, we can help unleash creativity in students and open doors to innovation. Learn more in the chapter resources page.

The Dynamic Learning Framework

Genius Hour: Genius Hour is an idea that comes to us from something called 20% Time at Google, where engineers are given 20 percent of their work time to work on passion projects that will benefit the company in some way. This idea has become very trendy in education and is coined as "Genius Hour." During Genius Hour, students are given a set period of time during school to explore their passions and interests and learn what they want to learn with a specific purpose. Genius Hour comes in many forms and flavors to fit the needs of a classroom, but it is a great strategy to go beyond the required content for your subject area and/or grade level. Learn more about Genius Hour in the chapter resources page.

Maker Projects: The Maker Movement has taken DIY to a whole new level, combining artistry, circuitry, and old-fashioned craftsmanship to create something new. Maker Spaces and Maker Projects focus on learning by doing. Students tinker, build, engineer, craft, program, and create with anything from cardboard to sophisticated technology. You don't need a fancy space filled with expensive equipment. You can start with something as simple as a Cardboard Challenge. Be sure to check out all of the additional ideas in the resources section of this chapter.

Entrepreneurial Learning: With little to no startup costs, online businesses can be started by just about anyone, including students. Help cultivate entrepreneurial skills like risk-taking, practicing the art of curiosity, perseverance, problem-solving, and taking ownership of the learning and enterprise. Developing these skills is important for all learners, not just those who take the entrepreneurial path. Remember, students can have moments of greatness before they leave our doors. With these skills, we can help our students blossom in new ways.

Try This: There are lots of digital tools to support design thinking, Genius Hour, Maker Projects, and entrepreneurial learning. Here are a few ideas:

- Use Google Drawings to brainstorm and create flowcharts.
- Use Google Keep to track progress.
- Use Blogger, Google Sites, social media, Flipgrid, or YouTube to share the story of the learning process.
- Use Google Forms for submitting project proposals.
- Use video tools like WeVideo, YouTube, or mysimpleshow to document the process and progress.
- Publish the final product or performance on a website for a global audience.
- Use Instagram, Google Photos, or other photo tools to document and share milestones.
- Use Google Drawings to draw a prototype.
- Use Google Docs to write a business plan.
- Use Google Sites or Blogger to create a business website.
- Create a YouTube channel to share business ideas, products, etc.

Beyond the Walls

Every student in every grade should have opportunities to connect and learn globally. I ask this question regularly across the county: "How many of you allow your students to publish online for a global audience?" The answer is almost always the same: Very few hands go up. Now flip that around. How many of you are bringing the outside world into your classroom through global collaboration, social media, video chats, and more? This is growing, but I don't think educators realize how easy it can be to connect their classroom to global resources. The possibilities are endless!

Strategies to Move Beyond the Walls

Publish Student Work for a Global Audience

As discussed in Chapter 12, giving students a global audience is a critical learning experience. There are many ways to implement this in the classroom. Depending on the age group and your school's policies, this may be something you as the teacher need to publish to protect their privacy. If unsure, ask your administrator. A good rule of thumb is to only publish first names with their work.

1. Choose publishing tools that offer not only a global audience, but some way to add comments or feedback. A blogging tool like Blogger, WordPress, Wix, or Weebly, or Edublogs will give you the commenting option. There are many other options besides blogging tools. Consider publishing on YouTube, Flipgrid, Google Sites, or even publishing a podcast.

2. Publish the work for the world! Don't hold back and limit the audience. Remember, students need exposure to feedback from other people besides teachers and parents.

3. Share with an intentional audience. Just because you published doesn't mean the right audience will find you. Share the link on social media with relevant experts. Use hashtags and your PLN to help you find the best audience.

Connect and Collaborate with Global Audiences

In Chapter 12, we discussed the importance of flattening the walls of your classroom and bringing the world to your students. There is no shortage of ways to connect and collaborate on a global scale. Many ideas were shared in Chapter 12, but here are some tips:

- What's the purpose? Start with the learning goals. What is the purpose of the connection? Let this guide your next steps.

- Who will connect (e.g., whole class, partners, groups)?

- With whom will you connect? Going back to those learning goals, do you want to connect with another classroom? Where? Or do you want to connect to an expert, author, or an organization like the San Diego Zoo?

- What tool(s) will you use? Whole class Google Hangout? Small groups collaborating on Flipgrid? Will you also use other tools to supplement the experience like Google Docs? If you teach students under the age of thirteen, your student options will be more limited. In that case, these may need to be teacher facilitated using your account.

Beyond the Tools

Think beyond using digital tools to complete only traditional assignments such as papers and reports. Use digital tools to do new things. Just going paperless or digital isn't enough. Use some of these new tools to go further, go deeper, and extend your students' learning. Reach beyond what you think a digital tool can do and should be used for, and challenge your students to demonstrate their learning in a new way.

Strategies to Move Beyond the Tools

Use Digital Tools to Do New Things

Almost all the ideas presented so far involve doing new things, but here are a few more ideas to get you going.

Using Digital Tools to GET Information Instead of Disseminate It

We often think of ways to deliver content using digital tools, which is fine, but getting students involved and interacting with content is better. Consider ways to open up your lessons to allow students to GIVE you information, check for understanding, feedback, comments, ideas, reflections.

Create Interactive Learning Experiences

Use digital tools that allow students to interact with the information in some way, like interactive graphic organizers, virtual manipulatives, interactive videos, and multimedia annotation.

Timely Feedback

Instant information at our fingertips means we can assess work and give students more timely feedback through comments, chats, and messaging systems.

Instant Collaboration

Collaboration between students can happen any time, any place. With collaboration tools like G Suite, it can be instant and synchronous so that students can work together in real time no matter the location.

I call Google Slides the Swiss Army Knife of the G Suite tools. It can be used for much more than just presentations. You can use it to create games,

FIGURE 15.4

interactive assessments, stop-motion video, eBooks, and more. Of course, Google Slides is just one example. We have no shortage of digital tools these days. Don't let yourself limit the tool's possibilities. Think beyond the tool's original purpose and how your students can get creative, and use new digital tools in unexpected ways.

Give Students Choice

Probably one of the best ways to explore this idea is to give students choice in creating and demonstrating their learning. This will open the door to not only more creative content but creative uses of digital tools. Don't automatically dismiss a tool because you don't think it's perfect for the job. Every time I have done this, a student has blown me away with an innovative use of digital tools. On the flip side, students also need to learn to let go and move forward when a tool isn't working. With our guidance, they can make these decisions while also realizing it's okay to take risks, even if they don't always pan out.

LIMITATIONS CAN PUSH CREATIVITY— AND SHAKE UP LEARNING!

For instance, sometimes less is more. Sometimes our limitations will help us see creative solutions that others fail to see. Embrace these limitations, as they just might lead to something new and innovative. In my early years of teaching, I was always trying new ways to integrate technology, but I wasn't going about it with purpose and meaning. I learned a very interesting lesson from a risk I took while teaching a unit on Edgar Allan Poe.

I had discovered a wonderful little Web-based comic strip maker. It was easy to use and didn't require creating accounts. I gave my students the task of retelling *The Tell-Tale Heart* using the comic strip maker. What could possibly go wrong? If you know anything about Edgar Allan Poe, you know that his writing is very dark and not necessarily something you would see conveyed in a comic strip. (Although there's a fabulous episode of *The Simpsons* that retells "The Raven.") This comic strip maker was actually very limited. You couldn't import any images; you were forced to use the small set of images available in the program. My students complained because they couldn't find the "perfect" image to represent the characters in the story. I told them they had to work with what was available and to get creative with the retelling of the story. I started worrying the limitations were going to make the projects a waste of time, but my students had invested too much time and energy for us to abandon the project, so I trudged on.

As students began to complete and print their projects, I noticed something amazing: *The Tell-Tale Heart* had become a comedy. As I mentioned, the character choices were limited. Several students chose a dinosaur image to represent the old man. They had, without even realizing it, completely changed the tone and mood of the story. Teachable moment! The project ended up being so creative and different that the principal asked to display my students' work in the hallway. It was one of my favorite projects that year.

The point to this story is that even when we plan carefully, we can miss the opportunities to be creative in new ways. If I had decided the tool was too simple and asked students to start over with something else, I would have lost their trust and the opportunity to completely shake up a classic story. Sometimes limitations scan force us to get more creative. Maybe you don't have a device for every student. Maybe your school won't purchase the tool you want. Maybe you don't have a lot of time to complete a project. Dig deep for some optimism, and use what you have when you have it. You won't know what you and your students are capable of if you never try!

Use Digital Tools for Formative Assessment, Not Just Summative

When technology became more widely available in schools, and a dedicated computer lab was all the rage, most used it as time to type a paper, do research, or create a PowerPoint or brochure. Today, with so much technology at our disposal, teachers can maximize digital tools to engage students throughout the learning cycle instead of focusing only on summative products. Even when we consider some of the more tangible products we have created in our classrooms—the tri-fold, the brochure, the diorama—they're still pretty static and finite. They're not the kinds of projects that grow and morph and inspire kids to keep learning. When we approach learning with a dynamic learning mindset and give students the freedom to create in their own way and to demonstrate the learning in their own way, we can move beyond a project like the diorama where you can run out of physical space, run out of ideas, and once you check the requirements off the list, it is done. And what if we don't have a one-and-done checklist? What if we allow students to meet, adjust, and expand their learning goals throughout the school year?

Beyond the Due Date

Allow students to continue work that interests them beyond the final assessment of an assignment or task. Thinking, learning, and exploring shouldn't be stifled simply because the submission deadline arrives. This idea might be the one that teachers struggle with the most. I agree students should learn to turn in their work on time, that is a life skill, but moving toward more

Dynamic Learning Experiences means moving away from the one-and-done mentality. Consider how dynamic today's workplace has become. We can immediately connect with colleagues across the globe, no matter the time zone. Many workplace projects are not one-and-done tasks. How many jobs do you know that require you to complete a worksheet every day? How many jobs give workers extra points for bringing in a box of Kleenex? Often the work environment is cyclical, like the school year, where we get to improve, try new things, and make revisions each year. Real-world learning doesn't end.

Have you ever had students so into their projects that they didn't want to turn them in? I have! And it would break my heart when I had to force them to stop so I could grade it. They had new ideas and other things they wanted to build or create. We must start turning those kinds of learning experiences into real opportunities. If we allow them to extend their work beyond the normal bounds of a one-and-done activity or worksheet, we are giving students opportunities to extend and enrich their learning, building a continuous learning mindset.

Strategies to Move Beyond the Due Date
Teacher Becomes Coach or Mentor

We know that our role as teachers has shifted. As facilitators of learning, we become the guide, the coach, even sometimes the mentor. As we support student learning past the due date, we become more of a mentor, encouraging exploration and creation without the bounds of a final test or assessment.

With many digital tools, learning can continue to take place even after an assignment has been turned in or assessed. For example, a Google Doc is a living document. It doesn't have to be forgotten in a folder somewhere. And it's not just G Suite tools, we must rethink the possibilities of our assignments when considering our new tools don't have the same limitations as paper. Students can continue to learn, create, and grow in different directions, going wherever their interests take them and using a variety of tools on a variety of devices that may be available. Yes, we still have to meet the assessment requirements and get those grades in the gradebook, but we can use the tools at our disposal to offer enrichment projects that support student learning past the due date.

Connect and Collaborate

As discussed in Chapter 7, Connect and Share, the value of connections and social learning can help students and teachers deepen their learning and forge collaboration partnerships. Help secondary students share their learning and projects with the outside world, beyond their friends and parents. Most middle school and high school students are very active sharers online, but they are not using these platforms to connect with the learning in class. Encourage ways to use social platforms for feedback and collaboration. This may be sharing a Twitter hashtag or a Facebook group relevant to their topic and interest.

Share Your Voice, Share Your Story

I am a firm believer in sharing your story, your reflections, and your journey, and this is something we can also cultivate in students. This is a different type of sharing than sharing for collaboration and feedback. This is about sharing something more personal: the story of your learning. Reflection is an important part of the learning process, and when you are bold enough to share an honest reflection about your fears, what went well, or where you failed, it helps students cultivate a growth mindset. They begin to understand that the process, the good, the bad, and the ugly, were all part of the learning journey. Help students to document their learning, reflect, and share with the world continuously.

Always Be Learning

A continuous improvement mindset can be difficult to instill in students who have been conditioned to due dates marking the end of the learning. Going beyond the due date also helps students become lifelong learners. Are they still curious about a topic? They can dig deeper into

FIGURE 15.5

Lesson Nutrition Facts

Serving Size: 45 minutes
Servings Per Class: 30

Amount Per Serving			
Learning Goals	5	Content Goals	4
Total Dynamic Learning Characteristics			2
Beyond the Bell			100%
Beyond the Grade Level & Subject			0%
Beyond the Walls			0%
Beyond the Tools			100%
Beyond the Due Date			0%
Creativity	50% •	Communication	5%
Critical Thinking	15% •	Collaboration	0%
Nutrition Grade B			

*Percent of Lesson is based on well-balanced classroom where students are exposed to a variety of dynamic learning experiences aligned with content area learning goals, and the ISTE Standards for Students. Your percent may be higher or lower depending on the needs of your students.

Shake Up Learning

the parts that interested them, the history, the problem-solving, or simply another question. Support and coach students. Help them see the importance of learning throughout the learning process and beyond.

As I began to cultivate examples of dynamic learning experiences and request ideas from my colleagues, I noticed a pattern. Most of them were choosing the same strategy, Beyond the Tool. It's a great place to start. Not all the dynamic learning characteristics are equal in impact. Some might be more difficult and challenging but also worth the investment and risk. Just start with one, then two, and slowly sprinkle in more dynamic learning characteristics throughout the year. The more characteristics you embed, the more dynamic the learning in your classroom can become. You won't use all of them in every lesson. That is pie-in-the-sky thinking, but you can use these strategies to push yourself and your students further out of your comfort zones as you build your skills as a dynamic learning designer and facilitator.

The Nutritional Value of Learning

I want you to think about your lesson plans like you are reading the nutritional facts on the back of a food product. If you want to give your classroom metabolism a nutritional boost, you must feed it the most nutritional, most Dynamic Learning Experiences that you can. If you just keep focusing on one healthy ingredient, you will not have a well-balanced classroom with well-balanced learning.

What is the nutritional value of the learning experiences in your classroom? Peel back the layers, not only how are you reaching the learning goals, but how all the pieces work together. Just like there isn't one perfect food that will deliver everything you need in one meal, there isn't one perfect learning experience that delivers everything students need. This is about finding the nutritional balance. Like we are told to eat the rainbow of veggies, we need to teach the rainbow.

Online Resources for Chapter 15

Here you will find resources mentioned in Chapter 15, supplemental resources, videos, as well as new and updated resources.

ShakeUpLearningBook.com/15

Discussion Questions

- What characteristics of dynamic learning do you already see in your classroom? What would you like to try?
- What percentage of the assignments in your classroom would you consider dynamic?
- Why do you think it is important to move from static learning to dynamic learning?
- How often do you integrate one of the Four Cs into your lessons?

Chapter 15 Actions

- Research one of the programs that interests you the most (e.g., Genius Hour, Maker Movement, Design Thinking). Refer to the links on the companion website if you need some resources.
- Plan one learning experience with a Dynamic Learning upgrade!
- Collaborate and discuss dynamic learning with another teacher or team of teachers face-to-face or online. Discuss your ideas, questions, limitations, and hopes.

The Dynamic Learning Framework

Reflection Space

_____

_____

_____

_____

_____

_____

_____

_____

_____

_____

_____

Notes

Robinson, Ken, "Do Schools Kill Creativity?" *TED*, Feb. 2006, www.ted.com/talks/ken_robinson_says_schools_kill_creativity.

Spencer, John, and A. J. Juliani, *Launch: Using Design Thinking to Boost Creativity and Bring Out the Maker in Every Student* (Dave Burgess Consulting, Inc, 2016).

THE HOW: EQUIPPING FOR IMPACT

One of the most impactful professional learning experiences of my teaching career was during my time at the Central Texas Writing Project Summer Institute. The Summer Institute is a professional development program conducted by all branches of the National Writing Project, where educators meet for four weeks to share and explore effective teaching strategies. Teachers who complete the institute become Teacher Consultants for the National Writing Project. The activity was called the "model lesson." We were required to deliver a lesson to the group of teachers as if they were our own students. It was a daunting assignment. It's one thing to learn alongside your peers and quite another to let them see you in action as a teacher and evaluate your performance. I learned so much about myself as a teacher that day. On the other days, when I was the student, I captured so many great ideas from teachers of all grade levels and experiences. It is unbelievably powerful to be in the seat of the student, to understand what it's like to experience a lesson from that side. We had all levels and subject areas in our institute, and you might wonder what high school teachers and kindergarten teachers can learn from each other. A lot, I tell you! You can learn valuable instructional strategies, facilitation strategies, questioning, and much more.

When I have the time, I love to use the model lesson experience in the workshops I teach. It is a very time-consuming activity that requires several days, but the value gained is well worth the time investment. Most professional learning opportunities just give you the why and the what, and sometimes they tell you the how, but it's rare that you get the time to do something with what you've learned and implement it in your classroom. That's why I spend so much time on planning and implementation in this book. I believe this portion of the book to be the most valuable. Please do more than just read. Plan, implement, reflect, and share!

This is the last piece of the pie, so to speak. In Part 3, we are going to discuss the last ring in the learning model before we create a Dynamic Learning Experience. I want you to have your toolbox loaded with ideas, tips, strategies, and more so you can create the best experience for your students. Together, we will dive into purposeful planning focused on learning outcomes. We will fearlessly implement it with finesse. We will reflect on our progress honestly and share our ideas with the world. Y'all ready for this?

Chapter 16
Purposeful Planning

Begin with the end in mind.
—Stephen Covey

As we work to find ways to make everything come together in our classrooms, we must remember the crucial step of planning. It's time to eat your veggies, y'all! This is where we put it all together. I have promised all along that this book is about action and change and not another sit-and-get book, and it's almost time for the fun part—implementation. But to implement, we must plan with purpose. Preparation is a key to success.

Lesson planning is nothing new, but if you struggle to find ways to integrate technology meaningfully, planning is the first step in making this a reality. If you work through the planning process with intention— and align it all with the learning needs of your individual students—you can approach dynamic learning with confidence, purpose, and meaning. The purpose of giving you a planning roadmap is not only to help you think through the process but also to get you to share your learning experiences with others.

I want to get you thinking about the entire process. For some of you, it might be a new approach. For others, it will serve as a good review. When you really begin to break down your plan,

you can see the gaps, the missing pieces, and the opportunities to become more dynamic.

Notice the lesson cycle in the last ring of the dynamic learning model:

FIGURE 16.1

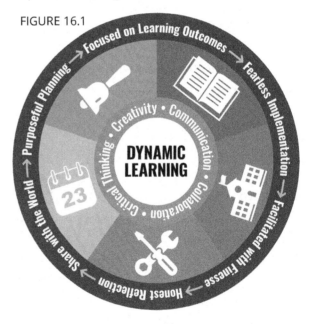

For the purposes of this book, I will not be using the term, "lesson plan," because I feel it is somewhat outdated; instead, I will use "Dynamic Learning Experience." As we move away from a traditional framework, we must also shift our vocabulary to help explain the shift in mindset. So "lesson plan" becomes "learning experience,"

"teacher" becomes "facilitator," and "student" becomes "learner."

Focused on Learning Outcomes

Renowned educator, author, and innovator, Stephen Covey, had it right in so many respects. Planning and prioritizing anything requires that we look ahead and determine what the end looks like, whether that is the end of a learning experience or a personal goal, such as running a marathon. Before you begin to integrate any of the ideas presented in this book, whether it has to do with technology or not, think about the end of the learning experience. What do you want your learners to discover, learn, and question? What are the learning goals?

Be goal oriented. Begin with your learning outcomes, not the technology. This is perhaps the most important tip of all. Everything we do as teachers should always come down to student learning and doing what's best for kids. Just because you are using technology doesn't insure you are meeting any objectives or standards. Is your *why* strong enough? If you cannot explain how the digital tool enhances or improves the learning experience, you are just using technology for technology's sake. If this is the case, start over!

Is your *why* strong enough?

Beginning with the desired learning outcomes is essential to insuring your learning experience will help you reach the end target. Before you start to plan, ask the following questions:

- What are the learning outcomes?
- What will learners learn and be able to do?
- Where do the Four Cs fit?
- Will this activity meet any of the ISTE Standards for Students?
- Do you want learners to create and publish online?
- What does the end of the experience look like?

I can't tell you how many conversations I've had with teachers that start with, "How can I use [insert digital tool name] in my classroom?" The question should never be how to fit this awesome new tool into your learning experience. The question is always, "What are the desired student outcomes?" Start with the concepts and skills you want your students to walk away with, and find the best tools to make that happen.

This approach can be a challenge, because sometimes it's easy to get distracted by technology—a shiny, new object that's cool and engaging but has little purpose. (Squirrel!) When this happens, the learning experience goes off course. Remember, each step, even the choice of specific tools, should move the learning arrow closer to the target! With today's prescribed curriculums and testing, we don't have time to waste, but we can learn how to use these tools to benefit our learners. Through the Dynamic Learning Experience, the learning becomes a journey, a story to tell.

Maybe the gears are already turning with ideas, or maybe you need some inspiration. Begin by brainstorming your favorite learning experiences. The lesson you are most proud of, the lesson you'd be happy to share with other teachers, the lesson that always goes well. Does it already include any dynamic learning characteristics? Or does it easily lend itself to a dynamic learning upgrade? Maybe your lesson involves learners creating something amazing, but it isn't shared. Could you give them an opportunity to publish for an intentional audience? Maybe it includes some passion topics or student choice that would allow learners to continue to work past the due date or final assessment. Or can you think of ways to help learners go beyond the bell and become lifelong learners? Have you thought about the possibility of making this interdisciplinary? Are there other subjects that could easily cross over into this learning experience? Could you collaborate with another teacher or group of teachers to create a learning experience that goes beyond your subject area or grade level curriculum?

Take a moment to brainstorm and use this space (if you like) to jot down ideas:

Practical Tips for Planning

As a digital learning coach and consultant, I give teachers practical tips for the classroom, and often I'm responding to the same repeated questions, dilemmas, and excuses. For those of you who have been integrating technology for a while, some of these might seem obvious. But we have too many teachers, even novice teachers fresh out of college, with no idea how to use digital tools to enhance student learning. With this book, I want to inspire you to push the boundaries of traditional learning, but I also want to keep it real and give you some ideas to shake up learning in your classroom. The following are a few digital learning tips any teacher can use in the classroom.

Get Technology into the Hands of Learners, Not Just Teachers

Modeling is great, especially when it comes to technology use, but it is far more important to get technology into the hands of learners. Often, and with good reason, teachers can become overprotective of the technology in their classroom. Sticky fingers and clumsy hands can make you resistant, particularly if a piece of equipment was purchased with your own money. But if you really want to see an impact, give your students a hands-on experience. Lay out the guidelines, show them proper use, then trust them. I see this a lot in one-iPad classrooms or even in classrooms with a single interactive white board. Teachers become super savvy with the new technology, and their learners are engaged and excited to see something new, but the overall learning stalls if students can't get their hands on the technology. Don't forget your purpose. Get technology into your learners' hands, even at the cost of giving up control.

Always Have a Plan B

No matter how much you prepare ahead of time for any lesson, even those not using technology, things don't always go as planned. We have all experienced those moments when technology doesn't cooperate—the Internet connection or Wi-Fi is down, the website you were using crashed, the video you were going to play is blocked. It happens to all of us. That is why it is crucial to not only think on your feet but to have a Plan B. It doesn't mean a completely new lesson plan, but it does mean knowing what you will do if the lesson just isn't working out. Sometimes you might go back to pen and paper. Other times you might rely on a tried-and-true tool such as Google Docs. Being flexible is nothing new for teachers, and integrating technology is no different. Be prepared to transition to Plan B before you lose an entire instructional period.

Get Organized

One of the best things you can do as a facilitator of digital learning is to organize information, directions, objectives, and resources online for your learners. Make life easier! Giving them **one** central location or website will make your life so much easier, and will allow learners to focus more time on their tasks. Provide just one link to write down, bookmark, link inside of Google Classroom, share with parents, whatever. I like to call this, "One link to rule them all," and a few always appreciate

my Lord of the Rings allusion. Multiple links confuse things. Use this central hub to contain all the links and information so it's organized in one place. This approach also keeps the learning experience as paperless as possible, which is a nice perk for any teacher. A central location serves as a one-stop shop, and it can take many forms, depending on the grade level, subject, and the digital tools at your disposal. A well-organized plan doesn't ensure success, but it sets a firm foundation.

In the primary grades, something simple like a Google Doc with directions and links works very well. Many primary teachers are fans of using Symbaloo to set up visual bookmarks. If you have a teacher website or blog, that could also work well for your learners and give you the flexibility to add different kinds of content. Make things even easier by bookmarking the link on their devices or shortening the URL so they can enter it with ease. If you are using mobile devices, a QR code to the central website can make your journey much easier.

Google Classroom is becoming a go-to resource for many Google-using educators to manage digital assignments and improve communication and collaboration. While Google Classroom might not give you the flexibility of a full website or blog, it is a great starting place for learners to get familiar with clicking on the link to find additional information and resources necessary for the assignment.

Don't forget that some of your more tech-savvy learners can offer other suggestions for website creation and sharing resources online. Encourage these learners to voice their input!

Here are some great tools for organizing your resources and assignments online:

- Google Classroom
- Google Sites
- Weebly
- Wix
- Blogger
- WordPress

Digital Workflow

Another advantage to digital assignments is the improved workflow. Teachers no longer have to shuffle home with stacks of papers to grade; they can assess digitally from anywhere. Anyone like me forget the stack of papers at school that you promised to have returned to students the next day? No more!

There are lots of learning management systems and assignment managers that can help with the entire workflow. I like Google Classroom. It's not as robust as some of the full learning management systems, but what it lacks in complexity, it makes up for in ease of use and organization. As students begin to work on their assignments, I can peek into their G Suite file to see how they progress, leave comments, and help them stay on track. Once it is turned in to the system, I can also communicate with students through private comments to help them improve their learning along the way.

Another bonus to using Google Classroom is the workflow is improved by saving your files in Google Drive. Once you create your first class in Google Classroom, the system automatically creates a folder in your drive. Within that folder are folders for each class, within each class folder are folders with each assignment and all the attached files. Everything is organized for you and your students.

If you are new to Google Classroom, I have a FREE online course to help get you started: shakeup.link/startgc.

The bottom line is to consider ways to improve your workflow, save time, and become more efficient!

Package Your Online Assignments

Save time and your sanity by packaging your online assignments! Don't miss out on one of the BEST things about blended learning and managing assignments online! Save yourself valuable instructional time and that oh-so-elusive teacher sanity by packaging your assignments so students have EVERYTHING they need in one place.

When you create an assignment online using your preferred tool, be that Google Classroom, Canvas, Edmodo, Blackboard, Google Docs, Google Sites, HyperDocs, whatever . . . give learners ALL the information online and in ONE place.

Give them detailed directions, the rubric, and the due date. Detail collaborative expectations, where and how to turn it in, what to do if they finish early, EVERYTHING you can think of they might need or for which they might ask! This will save you so much time answering questions. It is also very handy for absent work and demanding parents.

This is also documentation, a record of what is planned for your classroom. You can fine-tune it and revise as you see fit throughout the assignment.

Ten Things to Include in Your Digital Assignment Package:

Note: Not every assignment will require all ten of these, but this is a starting point that can help you think through the process.

1. **Give Each Assignment a Dedicated Number**

   This is an excellent tip for Google Classroom users that I learned from Alice Keeler; however, I think this advice can be useful no matter what platform you use. Numbers make it easier to search, find, and reference assignments. (Did you know the keyboard shortcut control/command + F will help you find words or numbers on a page?) I prefer three digits with the hashtag = #001. This makes it easy to find and organize in Google Drive, Google Classroom, or whatever platform you prefer.

2. **Include DETAILED Directions**

   Be as specific as possible! Leave nothing to chance or assume "they'll figure it out." Set your students up for success, and let them know exactly what you expect out of this assignment. If there are several steps, be sure to label "STEP 1, STEP 2," etc. For long-term assignments, consider creating assignment packages for each checkpoint so students know exactly what part is to be completed. What's great with a digital assignment is that you can add more details to this as new questions arise!

3. **Include Student-Friendly Learning Goals**

   Be sure you connect the assignment back to student-friendly learning goals so students understand the "why." Helping students make the connection between their assignment and their learning is very critical.

4. **Explain How the Assignment Will Be Assessed**

   There should never be any surprises for students. Be sure they understand exactly what you expect and how it will be assessed. If you have a rubric, all the better! Attach or link to the rubric to make the expectations crystal clear! If no rubric, be sure to explain in the directions how they will be assessed.

5. **Explain How Much Class Time Will Be Allotted**

   Will students be given class time to complete the assignment? If so, how long? Are they expected to complete the assignment outside of class? Again, be as specific as possible so there are no surprises like "I thought we were working on it in class today." (My students tried that one A LOT!)

6. **Include the Due Date (and Time)**

   This used to be one of my least favorite questions! I had to answer this question repeatedly. If the due date is in the assignment package, you should never have to answer that question again.

Purposeful Planning

Be sure to not only include the date but the time. Due at the beginning of class or at the end of class should be explicit in your assignment package. If you are using Google Classroom, it will "automagically" add the due date to the student's calendar. (BONUS: Guardian emails in Google Classroom will also allow parents to see due dates!

7. **Have Clear Collaboration Guidelines**

Collaboration doesn't magically happen just by saying you can work with a partner or a group. If students are collaborating with partners, groups, or outside of their class, be very specific about the guidelines and expectations. Who is responsible for turning in the work? Name a group leader and other roles as necessary. Explaining how they will be assessed individually will also be very important in collaborative activities.

8. **Explain the Turn-In Process**

Depending on what digital tools and learning management system you use, this will vary. I try to be as explicit as possible, like "don't forget to click the Mark as Done button in Google Classroom, or email the assignment to_____, or move it into the folder on the device," etc. Don't leave anything to question! Use screenshots and links to how-to documents when necessary. This is especially important with a new system or at the beginning of the year when students are learning your processes.

9. **What to Work on Next (Enrichment, Next Assignment, etc.)**

We all know students work at different paces. Some complete assignments faster than others. You may already have an excellent way to manage and differentiate for this. I like to preemptively answer these inevitable questions online in the assignment package. There seems to always be a student who asks, "Can we play games when we finish?" I usually have some go-to enrichment activities ready or a flexible learning path that will lead to the next assignment. This is also a great time for students to work on Genius Hour projects.

10. **Don't Forget to Include ALL Attachments and Links**

Remember, the point of assignment packaging is getting everything in ONE place. Your teacher life will be so much easier if you provide all the attachments and/or links necessary for the assignment, like templates, rubrics, research websites, digital tools, etc.

This may seem like a lot of extra work, but just like anything else, it will soon become a habit, and you can re-use your wording with minor adjustments in other assignments. In the long run, however, I think you will see how much time this can save you! Time saved from answering the same questions repeatedly and time saved explaining assignments to those who were absent.

Put a Bow on It! There's Your Assignment Package!

TIP: Save the text of your assignment packages in Google Keep or a Google Doc! This can serve as a template you can copy and paste and can save you time in the future.

Choosing Digital Tools

Given the impressive technology currently available to teachers, selecting the digital tools to work with can be a daunting task. As we discussed in Chapter 16, a good place to start is at the end. Think of the concepts and skills you want your learners to master, and choose the digital tools to get them there. Consider tools that can aid in the learning process and not merely to complete a cumulative task.

When you reach the point of choosing digital tools for your classroom, keep these tips in mind:

Don't Get Swept Away by the Next New Thing

I am guilty of this one. I am usually the first to sign up to try something new, but if you are always trying to integrate something new, you run the risk of focusing too much on the tool and not enough on the learning. Give new tools time to grow and evolve. Often you will find new tools that start off as free might suddenly require a fee the day you need to use it in the classroom. Or worse, the company didn't survive, and the tool is no longer accessible. New technology is part of what makes the twenty-first century so exciting, but always be cautious with a new tool that hasn't been proven or tested. It's smart to consider the source. Is it a new tool from a trusted company like Google or Apple, or was it released by a new company? Many teachers find out the hard way how tools can come and go. If the tool is in what's known as the beta testing phase, the company is still working out some kinks. I don't mind testing things out, but using tools in this phase isn't something I recommend for every teacher. When an app or website is less stable, it's more likely to crash or have glitches, so you might want to wait until it's out of beta.

Shop for Digital Tools Like You're on Amazon

With so many devices, digital tools, and gadgets for educators to choose from, it pays to be thorough and even a little picky. Shop as if you're on Amazon! In fact, you will likely find yourself on Amazon, the App Store, Google Play, or the Chrome Web Store. Read reviews, talk to friends, and take ideas from blogs and social media. Shopping is no longer a blind act. We can gather information on just about any idea or product, and we should find out what other teachers recommend. Ask about cost, effectiveness, and any glitches they may have encountered and how they were resolved. Gather as much information as you can before you ever click download. If you teach older students or have a teacher's aide, this could be a great research task for them!

Shop for Digital Tools Like You're on Amazon.

Purposeful Planning

Be Consistent

In the current climate, the temptation to try something new in the classroom every day is great, but learners need consistency. We have all known the frustration of investing extra time into a new tool and having it disappoint. Risk-taking with new tools is great but not appropriate every day. To make the most of your instructional time, stick with the dependable tools your learners already know how to use. Sprinkle in the new stuff every now and then. You don't want your classroom to be so unpredictable that learners start to feel lost. While you don't want to become mundane, consistency does allow for in-depth learning and gives students the opportunity to grow more adept at using specific digital tools. Balance is key.

Don't Integrate Too Many Tools at Once

Resist the urge to integrate too many different digital tools at the same time. App-smashing is fun when done with purpose, but if you try to do too much at once, you risk shifting the focus to the tool and using technology for technology's sake. If you love tech like I do, it can be easy to keep adding more ideas and tools to your lesson. But integration should happen gradually. Build your students' digital toolboxes over time. It doesn't have to happen in one day.

Through purposeful planning that is guided by the learning goals, we can transform the learning in our classroom. It's not always fun, but we can all support each other by sharing ideas, strategies and tips, like the ones shared in this chapter. You know the learners in your classroom better than anyone. Trust your gut and plan something dynamic!

Online Resources for Chapter 16

Here you will find resources mentioned in Chapter 16, supplemental resources, videos, as well as new and updated resources.

ShakeUpLearningBook.com/16

Discussion Questions

- How are you getting the technology into the hands of your students?
- Does your school allow students to publish online to a global audience? If not, find out why! If so, how are you letting your students go global?
- How often do you find yourself going to plan B, C, or D?
- Do you have a central hub for students to use as their one-stop shop for your class? If so, how has it worked? If not, what's holding you back?
- How do you package your digital assignments? In your experience, what have been the most important details to include?

- Think about how you select digital tools for use in your classroom. How can you improve your selection process?
- Have you ever had a lesson involving technology that frustrated you? What did you learn from that experience?
- What is the most difficult part of technology integration for you?

Chapter 16 Actions

- Brainstorm some ideas for a lesson you would like to try. Ask yourself these questions:
  - o What are the learning outcomes?
  - o What will learners learn and be able to do?
  - o Where do the Four Cs fit?
  - o Will this activity meet any of the ISTE Standards for Students?
  - o Do you want learners to create and publish online?
  - o What does the end of the experience look like?
- Build a classroom website, if you don't already have one, using the digital tool of your choice.
- Try Google Classroom! It's a great way to manage digital assignments and increase communication and collaboration. Check out my resources for tips, tricks, e-books, and more at shakeup.link/gclass.
- Create a digital assignment with your students, and package all of the details. Share your links and reflection on Twitter with #ShakeUpLearning, or in the Shake Up Learning Facebook Group (shakeup.link/community).
- Share one thing you learned in this chapter with a colleague who struggles with technology use.
- Go app fishing! Spend some time exploring and researching the best apps for your classroom. Here are a couple places to start: For Chrome Apps, go to shakeup.link/chromedb, and for iOS Apps, shakeup.link/appfishing. Share your findings on Twitter with the #ShakeUpLearning hashtag or in the Facebook Group.
- Is there a teacher in your school who always seems to have the best ideas or luck when using tech with kids? Ask that teacher for tips and advice for your classroom.

Reflection Space

Chapter 17
Facilitating with Finesse

I never teach my pupils; I only attempt to provide
the conditions in which they can learn.
—Albert Einstein

As you plan, it is important to also think about how you will facilitate the learning. What actions will you take? What strategies will you use? When the classroom gets messy and chaotic, some teachers feel as if they are losing control, but as I mentioned earlier, it is entirely possible to manage this aspect of dynamic learning with a few key strategies and, yes, finesse!

So before we actually design your Dynamic Learning Experience, let's discuss some tips for facilitation.

Let Go

Remember how we are trying to get comfortable with being uncomfortable? As teachers, this means stepping out of the way and letting our learners take some risks, stretch their creative legs, and learn to solve their own problems. Of course, this is easier said than done. A good way to start is posing thought-provoking questions designed to lead them down a path of discovery. Resist the urge to spoon feed them the answer. Some of the most surprising and innovative projects come about when we just let go!

The "Yes, and . . . ?" Approach

This strategy comes from the improv community. As students begin brainstorming and trying to find creative solutions to problems, use the "Yes, and . . . ?" approach. When a student shares an idea or thought, teachers and students respond with, "Yes, and . . . ?" This forces the student to keep going deeper and thinking of other options, connections, and scenarios that may be better and more innovative. Repeat as they continue to dive deeper.

The "Yes, and . . . ?" approach in the classroom forces teachers and learners to be more positive and collaborative and stop saying no to ideas they don't understand. This strategy also promotes active listening. Try this in collaborative projects where learners are problem-solving together. Try this as a facilitator to help guide and add ideas without negating a student's original ideas or thought process.

The Art of Knowing When to Switch Gears

When you are invested in your own learning, you want to see your investment pay off. I've seen teachers give up on an assignment just because the technology didn't work as they wished or took longer than expected. That's a risk you must be willing to take. If you abandon a project in which learners have already invested, they will lose trust in you. Give them room, and accept that things might not go the way they were planned. As teachers, we learn to be flexible in many different capacities. Technology is no different. Be flexible and ready to learn and adjust as needed, just as you do with any lesson plan.

Resist the Urge to Do Everything for Your Learners

As teachers, we serve. We want to help. We want to do everything we can for our learners. Sometimes we do too much. We answer too many questions and do the hard work for them. This kind of service doesn't do your students any favors, so resist the urge. Don't Google for them. Don't curate for them. Show them how to do it for themselves. They need these skills. You might think it will save time and free them up to do another task, but remember that finding the information is a skill they will need in the workplace, and hand-holding will only deprive them of a marketable skill.

Ask Three Before Me

Teachers often become the keeper of the knowledge, the official question answerer, the first place that learners go for help with everything. That's a huge burden, especially when you're juggling countless other tasks in the classroom on any given day. Encourage your learners to rely more on each other during class. Make sure they know it's okay to not only collaborate but also to ask one another for help when they get stuck or have a question. The ask-three-before-me strategy is brilliant and has saved me a lot of time. It can be used in a number of collaborative settings that might or might not involve technology. The greatest benefit is that it frees up a teacher to focus on facilitating the learning. In my classroom, I would often deliver small-group instruction while the rest of the class worked on other assignments, stations, or learning menus. It became difficult to manage questions while I was working with my small group. Some learners just naturally go to the teacher with every little question, and often these questions can be answered by other learners in the classroom or found online. The ask-three-before-me rule helped teach my students how to work together to solve problems and answer questions while completing their assignments. This strategy works especially well when digital tools are involved. (TIP: You can also make YouTube and/or Google Search one of the "three" options to ask for help.)

Don't Be Afraid to Let Your Students Teach You

Our students have a lot of knowledge and skills, especially when it comes to technology. Long gone are the days of the teachers being the gatekeepers of knowledge. It's okay if you don't know the answer when it comes to the technology, and students will love the chance to help teach you. As you are designing your learning experience, and you wonder about how a digital tool works or if there's an app for that, ask your students!

Even if they do not know the answer, they will be willing to help you figure it out. Another thing I love about talking to students about technology is they always show me some new app, some new trick or shortcut my adult world hasn't seen yet. A lot of our students have their fingers on the pulse of what's hot, and while that might not always be of value in the classroom, sometimes it can be a huge benefit. Don't immediately dismiss a tool because you think it isn't educational. Pokémon Go, or whatever the latest tool is, will prove you wrong every time!

Utilize Student Tech Experts

It's misguided to assume every student is comfortable with technology. This country still has a large digital divide. Still, it's likely there are experts in your classrooms that can help bridge that gap. Not only should you use those tech-savvy students to help you learn new digital skills, you should also use them as go-to experts for other students. This can be a very empowering experience for students. It can help those with inclinations toward technology to further explore their passions, and it can definitely help get more girls and young women interested in technology.

I've seen this approach used several different ways in the classroom. Depending on how many tech-savvy students you have, you could establish a permanent role or group or even a rotating job for students in your class. Keep in mind you don't want to force this role on any student who is uncomfortable or shy. At least initially, it should be used on a volunteer basis. You can even have an application process if you have enough interest. Whatever route you take, encourage students with potential, and help them hone their leadership skills. This idea can even be taken a step further by establishing a student help desk, genius bar, or Chrome Squad for your school.

Don't Assess the Bells and Whistles—Content Is King

Technology can inject excitement into students' projects, but when it's time to assess their work, remember to go back to your original learning goals. What was the purpose of the lesson? Was it to include three animations in a PowerPoint? I hope not! The fun little extras (the bells and whistles) can add something special to a project, but they're never the end goal. Steer clear of rubrics that rely strictly on numbers—such as the number of slides, videos, or photos included; instead, use a rubric that focuses on the content and skills the lesson was designed to teach. Step back and allow your students to surprise you. They just might demonstrate their learning in a new and unexpected way!

Ann Witherspoon, Instructional Technologist in Midlothian ISD and participant in my Dynamic Learning Workshop, asks, "Is the rubric for the teacher or the student?" I think this is a great question as we ponder how to assess the learning and the use of rubrics. Most of the rubrics I have seen were designed to help a teacher grade, not assess, for learning.

Use Checkpoints to Monitor Progress and Provide Meaningful Feedback

We all get off track from time to time. It's important, particularly with long-term projects, to give students checkpoints or milestones along the way. I learned this the hard way in my classroom. I might have visually observed the work taking place in class, but if I didn't take the time to confer with my students and insure they were on the right path, the final product was often far off. That was my fault. Remember to monitor progress and discuss learning goals throughout the entire project. Students need reminders at every grade level!

Peer Feedback

Remember that peer feedback can be just as meaningful—sometimes more powerful—than a response from the teacher. This can be verbal, although some students will struggle with verbal feedback. Online feedback through something like comments in a Google Doc tends to get the more reluctant students (i.e., the ones who won't share aloud) to share, collaborate, and give feedback to other students.

I like the "TAG" strategy to get them started. T for tell the creator something you like. A for ask the creator a question. G for give the creator a positive suggestion. This strategy is short enough that it doesn't seem too daunting but can help get them engaged in the content. The burden of feedback doesn't have to fall solely on the teacher. Remember to get kids communicating about their work.

The role of facilitator requires that we take a step back and put the learning in the hands of our students. This is sometimes easier said than done, but with utility belt of strategies and tips like the ones shared in this chapter, you can light the path for your students!

Online Resources for Chapter 17

Here you will find resources mentioned in Chapter 17, supplemental resources, videos, as well as new and updated resources.

ShakeUpLearningBook.com/17

Discussion Questions

- How do you balance the art of facilitation? How do you guide them without directing them too much?
- Have you ever had to abandon a lesson because the technology wouldn't cooperate? Explain. What would you do differently?
- What are your favorite strategies for facilitations? Please share on Twitter with the #ShakeUpLearning hashtag or in the Facebook Group shakeup.link/community.
- In what ways could you make use of the student tech experts in your classroom?
- How do you give feedback on digital assignments? Where do you see room for improvement?

- How do you assess digital work? What is something you would like to change or improve in this process.
- How do you monitor progress on long-term projects?

Chapter 17 Actions

- Try one of the facilitation strategies from this chapter in your next lesson.
- Create a tech expert role or team for your classroom or school to both empower students and help you focus on facilitation. (Check out the Chrome Squad resources on the companion website.)
- Create a rubric for a digital assignment that is designed to assess the content or skills for that particular unit or lesson. Try to avoid adding things like the number of slides required.
- Try the TAG strategy for peer-to-peer feedback:

  T - Tell the creator something you like.

  A - Ask the creator a question about their work.

  G - Give the creator a suggestion for improvement.

Reflection Space

Chapter 18

What Does Dynamic Learning Look Like?

If you don't know where you are going,
you'll end up someplace else.
—Yogi Berra

We have covered a lot of ground! A lot! We've talked about our why, we've talked about the what, and now we are working on the how—how to design and implement Dynamic Learning. But if you are like me, I tend to get irritated when people don't give me complete examples of what things are supposed to look like when you put it together. It's sort of like putting together a bookshelf from IKEA: You need the full picture. So in this chapter we are going to take a deeper look at some Dynamic Learning Experience examples, model lessons if you will. All of the model lessons, including links to directions, templates, and more can be found in this chapter's resource page: shakeuplearningbook.com/18.

Examples and Commentary
Models and Equations in Google Sheets by Christine Pinto

- BEYOND the Tools
- Grades Pre-K through Second Grade

Learning Outcomes

- Students will be able to create equations that equal five, ten, or twenty.
- Students will be able to decompose a number and understand the purpose of the equal sign.
- Students will gain a foundational understanding for multiplication.
- Students will be able to write mathematical expressions.

In this learning experience designed for littles, Christine Pinto, kindergarten teacher and coauthor of *Google Apps for Littles*, uses Google Sheets templates to help her students learn basic addition and give them early exposure to equations. Students can "make five," "make ten," or "make twenty," following the colors in the Google Sheets cells.

The kids make their models by using single digit numbers according to the color key to color the cells. First, they fill in the blank cells with a color by typing the number that corresponds to the color. For example, they could fill three boxes with green, two with orange. Then they add their equation to the yellow box to show how it makes five: three green plus two orange equals five. Then they check their answer in the blue box following the example in FIGURE 18.1.

FIGURE 18.1

	Using 2 colors only, how many ways can you make five? Create a model using the five frame											
	0	1	2	3	4	5	6	7	8	9		
							Type an equation in the yellow box to match your model.					
							Check your answer in blue box. =___+___					

ISTE Standards for Students

- Empowered Learner
- Computational Thinker
- Creative Communicator

Which of the Four Cs did students use and cultivate?

- Critical Thinking

How is this learning experience dynamic?

This example at the very least is going beyond the tool. Spreadsheets are a tool designed to analyze data. Instead of entering data in a spreadsheet, students are creating, developing, and demonstrating an understanding of composing five, ten, or twenty by using arrays. It illustrates how Google Sheets can be used to create an interactive math experience. Most primary students are not exposed to Google Sheets. Heck, a lot of adults still don't know how to use a spreadsheet application, but Christine illustrates so vividly, yes the littles can!

I think this learning experience can easily go beyond grade and subject level depending on what you teach by helping students gain a deeper understanding of math, equations, and even how to use Google Sheets to calculate formulas.

No matter the age or subject you teach, I feel this learning experience can open your eyes to what you thought was possible with sheets with littles or with any group of students that you think may face barriers to learning. In *Google Apps for Littles*, Christine Pinto proves that, yes, they can! Never underestimate your students!

Creating Comics with Google Slides
by Sylvia Duckworth

- BEYOND the Tools
- Any grade level
- Any subject

Learning Outcomes

Students will learn how to tell a story collaboratively through comic strips using Google Slides and the Bitmoji Chrome extension.

What Does Dynamic Learning Look Like?

Using comic strips to tell a story can be a powerful way for students to connect the learning and deepen their understanding, and, well, they are just plain fun! In this lesson, Sylvia Duckworth, author of *Sketchnotes for Educators*, shows you step-by-step how to create a comic strip in Google Slides, and how to use the fun Bitmoji extension. If you haven't used Bitmoji, it's a fun, personalized avatar creator that lets you create versions of yourself in different costumes, outfits, situations, and reactions, like emojis on steroids!

ISTE Standards for Students

- Empowered Learner
- Digital Citizen
- Knowledge Constructor
- Creative Communicator
- Global Collaborator

Which of the Four Cs did students use and cultivate?

- Collaboration
- Creativity

How is this learning experience dynamic?

Sylvia's learning experience definitely helps us find new ways to use tools like Google Slides as a comic strip creator and digital storytelling tool. As I mentioned in my earlier story about using comic strips to retell *The Tell-Tale Heart* by Edgar Allan Poe, there are often unexpected ways that digital storytelling can help students connect their learning with visuals. The options for telling a story with comic strips, or other digital storytelling tools, are limitless. Students could be retelling a story, novel, historical event, or they could be writing their own stories and bringing them to life.

FIGURE 18.2

Wild Learning with Roz
by Sean Fahey, Karly Moura, Michele Waggoner, Heather Marshall, and Becky Ogbouma

- BEYOND the Subject and Grade
- BEYOND the Walls
- BEYOND the Tools
- Grades 4-5
- Subject: ELAR

Learning Outcomes

- Students will understand and demonstrate how characters are transformed through their relationships with others.
- Students will be able to determine the theme of the story and summarize text.

This HyperDoc has it all, y'all! It is designed to help students dig deeper into *The Wild Robot* by Peter Brown. This is actually much more than just a Dynamic Learning Experience, this is a dynamic learning unit! Through this unit, students complete independent and collaborative activities through various tools to build vocabulary, summarize text, respond to literature, and complete STEM connected activities. This experience is very interactive, including things like video responses using Flipgrid, Padlet, Seesaw, and creating Booksnaps, a visual way to connect to your reading, created by Tara Martin.

Keep in mind, this group shared an entire unit. You can also use the template for individual lessons within a unit. Because this is an entire unit of activities, this also helps reach more of the beyonds for dynamic learning. Remember, your goal is just to push you and your students further. You do not have to check every box on every assignment. Remember to keep it practical and doable for where you are.

The creators also shared a week-by-week teacher's guide to show you exactly what to do. Even if you don't teach this novel, this lesson will inspire you with ideas for any subject or grade.

ISTE Standards for Students

- Knowledge Constructor
- Creative Communicator

Which of the Four Cs did students use and cultivate?

- Communication
- Collaboration
- Critical Thinking
- Creativity

How is this learning experience dynamic?

Because this learning experience was designed to accompany the Global Read Aloud (GRA) activity, it went completely beyond the walls of the classroom. By participating in the GRA and using the HyperDoc, students were collaborating with other students across the globe. The use of Padlet and Flipgrid also allows students to publish to a larger audience.

This learning experience also goes beyond the language arts subject area with the additions of the STEM activities. These activities allow students to problem-solve, build, and connect to the science, engineering, and math they were reading about in the book.

This lesson takes a standard presentation tool, Google Slides, and turns it into a series of packaged learning materials in the form of a HyperDoc. Google Slides are used again to

What Does Dynamic Learning Look Like?

FIGURE 18.3

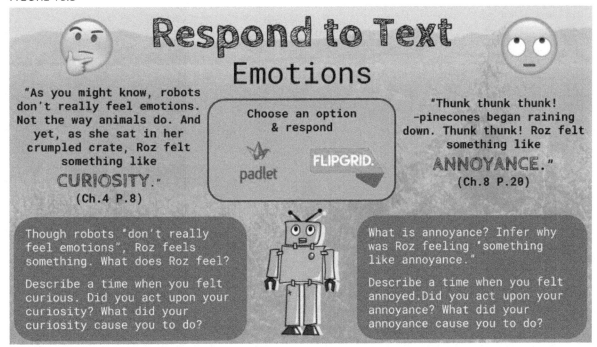

create a collaborative classroom dictionary. Creating Booksnaps using SnapChat, Seesaw, or Google Drawings allow students to go beyond the intended use of the tool and create visuals that represent their thinking of the text. The simple website builder, Google Sites, is used to create a digital breakout game as a collaborative problem-solving activity to wrap up the unit in a fun and exciting way.

#Goaltime by Matt Hawkins

- BEYOND the Walls
- BEYOND the Bell
- BEYOND the Grade Level and Subject Area
- BEYOND the Due Date
- Grades 2-6
- English Language Arts, Social Students, Math, Science

Learning Outcomes

- Students will be able to write a personal learning goal.
- Students will learn how to use technology and information to guide their own path toward their own learning goal.

#Goaltime is a Genius Hour inspired learning unit. Students set their own goals and share the learning process with the school community and beyond. Goals include deep dives into personal interests and projects that aim to help someone or solve a problem. Scaffolding includes guided project brainstorming and proposals with a sharing session at the end that can include showcases or presentations.

The #goaltime learning experience includes three main projects that are completed through-out the year that utilize the Genius Hour Launch

FIGURE 18.4

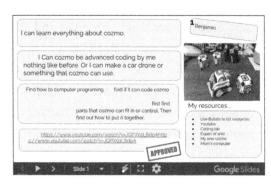

What Does Dynamic Learning Look Like?

Cycle developed by A.J. Juliani and John Spencer, authors of *Launch*. The first project is a passion project and can include any personal interest. In later projects, students must solve a problem or help someone else.

At the end of each project, students share what they have learned in different ways. Past sharing has included a student showcase, stand up presentations, Shark-Tank-style pitches, and video narrations of their presentation slides. Matt has compiled examples of students' presentations in a Google Site and shared those with the world! It's so powerful seeing students share, especially something they are passionate about. (Check them out in the chapter resources page.)

ISTE Standards for Students

- Empowered Learner
- Digital Citizen
- Knowledge Constructor
- Innovative Designer
- Computational Thinker

Which of the Four Cs did students use and cultivate?

- Communication
- Collaboration
- Critical Thinking
- Creativity

How was this learning experience dynamic?

This learning experience manages to hit all of beyonds, but please accept that this is rare and not an expectation. Genius Hour types of activities have a way of helping us really move beyond traditional learning. Because this activity helps students explore their passions, set their own goals, and create a continuous learning mindset, it definitely helps move us beyond the bell. Since students taking part in #goaltime are also sharing their work with the world, they are moving beyond the walls. They could also be collaborating with outside experts. And the topic of choice may very well take them outside the prescribed curriculum for their given grade level or subject. As students continue to learn, grow, create, and extend the project throughout the school year and perhaps further, they are really beginning to see learning past the due date. The use of tools very much depends upon the project, but students can easily move into using new tools to do new things as they research, learn, create, perform, etc.

Project Wonder by Carrie Baughcum

- BEYOND the Bell
- BEYOND the Walls
- BEYOND the Grade Level and Subject Area
- BEYOND the Due Date
- BEYOND the Tools
- K-8th grade
- Special Education
- English Language Arts, Social Students, or Science

Learning Outcomes

- Students will recognize moments of wonder and be able to formulate a question to reflect what they do not know or understand about the world around them.
- Students will demonstrate, implement and perform an inquiry and research process.
- Students will demonstrate, implement and perform media literacy skills, find reliable

sources for school reports (both on- and offline), and become a smart consumer of products and information.

- Students will use researched information and apply it to the writing process (principles to writing paragraphs): Write clear topic sentences, exhibit effective unity, support, coherence, and mechanics in paragraphs, write in order to satisfy the reader's understanding, evaluate their own writing, use information technology in production of writing assignments.

- Students will understand the preparation and presentation skills needed for oral communication in an informal sharing session, as both a speaker and a listener.

- Students will develop listening skills, articulate and enunciate words and sentences clearly and efficiently, show confidence and clarity in speaking projects, and demonstrate ability to share information to articulate and share learning with others.

Wonder and curiosity are everywhere. Life, learning, and new experiences can create all kinds of questions and wonder for our students. With each moment of wonder, we have two choices: let the moment pass or grab hold of it, embrace it, and use it to guide, teach, and empower our students to be fearless learners. Carrie's Project Wonder provides the structure, routine, tools, information, and strategies for providing one, a few, or infinite moments of exploration for your students while developing skills that will enable and empower them to be independent, lifelong learners.

This learning experience echoes many of the ideas found in Genius Hour, but is more guided, helping students explore and research the topics that interest them and convey their findings through writing. I love how she designed this experience! Carrie teaches special education and is constantly proving that her students are capable of greatness.

ISTE Standards for Students

- Empowered Learner
- Creative Communicator

Which of the Four Cs did students use and cultivate?

- Communication
- Critical Thinking

How is this learning experience dynamic?

This learning experience helps cultivate lifelong learning and gives students an opportunity to research the things that they are curious about, which helps us go beyond the bell and build that mindset.

Since the topics are open, students can explore ideas that go beyond their normal grade level and subject area curriculum.

Project Wonder also helps us see beyond the due date, and we use this as a project to continue throughout the year, not just focused on an end assessment.

Students can use and explore a wide variety of tools and use them in new ways to process learning and create.

More examples can be found in the Dynamic Learning Experience database,

FIGURE 18.5

FOLLoW YOuR CuRIoSiTY
PROJECT WONDER 2017–2018

1)	**TAKE NOTES** Using the Project Wonder question you selected *(it does not have to be a question you created)*, use Google Search/Online Library Resources gather facts from trusted and reliable sources, that will be used to answer your Question. Write your notes / facts below
2)	**DOCUMENT SOURCES** Record and document the trusted and reliable sources supporting /answering your wonder
3)	**ORGANIZE NOTES** Copy and paste your facts into the [*insert writing organizer you use in your class*]
4)	**DRAFT YOUR PARAGRAPH** [*insert writing organizer / paragraph writing process you use in your class*]
5)	**FINAL DRAFT** Use the Self Edit Checklist to get your final draft ready to share
6)	**SHARE** Be ready to use this information to share your Project Wonder learning during group discussion

shakeup.link/DLdatabase. It is searchable and filterable, and when you are ready, you can share your own!

After you examine the ideas in these examples and the general style and delivery of the dynamic learning experiences, think about your classroom. What ideas would you like to try? Jot down your ideas below:

_____

_____

_____

Online Resources for Chapter 18

Here you will find resources mentioned in Chapter 18, supplemental resources, videos, as well as new and updated resources.

ShakeUpLearningBook.com/18

Discussion Questions

- What did you like about the learning experience examples?
- What is one idea from these examples you are willing to try?
- What is the hardest part of planning of lesson?

Chapter 18 Actions

- Reflect on the learning experience examples and brainstorm a list of three to five ideas you want to try.
- Bookmark the Dynamic Learning Experience database and revisit often for fresh inspiration.
- Thinking ahead: Reach out to a colleague or teacher friend and ask them to collaborate with you on your Dynamic Learning Plan coming up in the next chapter.

Reflection Space

What Does Dynamic Learning Look Like?

Chapter 19
Your Dynamic Learning Plan

A goal without a plan is just a wish.
—Antoine de Saint-Exupéry

Now that you have done some pre-planning and seen some examples of Dynamic Learning Experiences, let's start working on YOUR PLAN. You can do this on your own, collaborate with a partner, or work with your team. There is room to write in this book if you prefer to handwrite. I've also created a Google Doc at shakeup.link/DLplan for you to copy and write your plan digitally. Use this document to brainstorm!

1. Identify desired results. (Always start here!)
- What are the big ideas we want learners to understand and use?
- What unit of study are you currently planning or will be planning soon?
- What are your learning targets?

2. Pose essential questions for the learning experience.
- What provocative questions will foster inquiry, understanding, and transfer of learning? Learn more about essential questions at shakeup.link/essques.
- What questions can you ask students to help them focus on important aspects of the topic?

3. Determine assessment evidence.
- How will we know learners have understood the big ideas? How will you know they "get it"?

4. Plan learning experiences and instruction.
- What learning activities will facilitate understanding of the big ideas?

5. Determine the necessary technology for learning.
- Will you use technology? How will technology enhance and support the learning of the above learning targets?

6. Set dynamic learning goals.
- How will you make this learning experience more dynamic?
- How can you step out of your comfort zone and take risks?
- Will the learning experience be student centered? How will it be authentic? Set some goals for yourself!
- How will this lesson extend beyond a normal one-and-done activity? What opportunities will learners have to continue the learning?

- Be specific on how learners will communicate, collaborate, and extend the learning.

DLE Planning Template

Because I want this book to be truly effective, the challenge in this chapter is perhaps the greatest.

It's time to step into action. Below is the Dynamic Learning Experience Planning Template that will help you plan your learning experience. You can submit your learning experience and be able to view all the other lessons that have been shared in the Dynamic Learning Experience Database, which is searchable.

MYTH BUSTING THE EXCUSES

Are any of the following issues circling in your head right now?

How can I do these things on top of everything else that is required of me as a teacher?

I don't have time for this.

I don't have one-to-one devices, so this will not work in my classroom.

Let's take a moment to reflect on what may be holding you back. As I mentioned earlier, mindset is not only a hot buzzword, but also a real affliction that can hold anyone back from doing anything. Do you feel negative thoughts about the ideas presented so far? If so, take a moment to reflect on why you feel negative about these ideas. Is it because you were required to read this book, and you feel like it was a waste of time? Or do you feel like it really isn't something you are prepared for? Do you need more guidance, more training so that you can feel comfortable going forward? Remember, we aren't aiming for comfort. If you are always in your comfort zone, you are limiting your potential as a teacher.

I understand that teaching isn't easy. I've been teaching for over fifteen years. I may have yet to see it all, but I've seen a lot, and I've heard every excuse in the book from students and teachers. Yes, I know most of you have a prescribed curriculum you must adhere to in order to meet the demands of your school system and administration requirements. But I ask you this: Where is the wiggle room? Where can you try one new thing? Can you teach your curriculum and reach your learning goals in a new way? What if trying new things meant you found a new way to reach learners, even cover more of your required curriculum in less time? Would you try it then? Don't assume this is going to be more work, more time, and cause problems. Stretch the possibilities! Flexibility is key! You will never have perfect, pie-in-the-sky scenarios. Even the richest schools will share your complaints. There is always more to aspire to, more to obtain, more to upgrade. Upgrade your teaching first and turn your struggles into strengths!

Your Dynamic Learning Plan

We are all better together, but I do ask those who take an idea from this collection of lessons to also contribute a lesson. Give one; get one.

I encourage users to complete all fields for your first plan. The more information you share, the easier it is for another teacher to follow. Download the Google Doc template and access the submission form at shakeup.link/DLEform.

Name(s):

Title:

School District/Campus (or Employer):

Blog or Website:

Twitter Handle:

THE DYNAMIC LEARNING EXPERIENCE

Name of Learning Experience:

Grade Level(s):

Content Area(s):

Length of Learning Experience:

Summary:

Learning Outcomes:

STANDARDS

Content Area Standards: (CCSS, TEKS, whatever the standards are in your state or country)

ISTE Standards for Students:

Which of the Four Cs Did Students Use and Cultivate?

Please Explain How the Four Cs Chosen above Were Integrated in This Learning Experience.

DYNAMIC LEARNING CHARACTERISTICS

In What Ways Was This Learning Experience *dynamic*?

☐ BEYOND the Bell   ☐ BEYOND the Tools

☐ BEYOND the Grade & Subject   ☐ BEYOND the Due Date

☐ BEYOND the Walls

Explain Each of Your "Beyond" Selections above:

IMPLEMENTATION

Required Materials, Equipment, Digital Tools, and Resources for the Learning Experience

What devices are needed or recommended? What digital tools did you use? Did you need to create accounts? Any tips for other teachers? Please share.

Instructional Plan (Step-by-Step)

This is the entire, step-by-step process. Write this as if you are giving to another teacher to deliver in their classroom.

Facilitation Strategies

How did you guide and facilitate this learning experience? What strategies did you use and how (i.e. utilize student experts, ask three before me, etc.)?

Differentiation

Did you differentiate content, product, or process of this learning experience? Did you offer student choice? If so, please explain and share.

Quality Feedback

How did you give quality feedback to students during the experience?

Assessment

How did you assess this lesson or activity? How will you know when they get it? Rubric?

Student Work Samples

Additional Links and Resources

REFLECTION

Please share a brief reflection about the implementation of this learning experience. What went well? What would you change? (You may share this as a text paragraph or share a link to a video reflection, sketch note, or however you choose to reflect.)

- What went well (start off with the positive)?
- What didn't go well?
- What would you change?
- Was it dynamic?
- How was it different from other learning experiences you have facilitated in the past?
- Feel free to add any other comments, suggestions for other teachers, or fun anecdotes.

COMMENTS

Please feel free to add any additional information, directions, or comments for teachers interested in this lesson.

After completing the template—but before you implement—share it with a colleague, a teacher friend, another educator, or on social media or the Shake Up Learning community for ideas and feedback. An outside perspective can often help you think of things you may have not considered. Teachers are always full of tips and advice and ready and willing to help. I promise it's worth the extra time!

Online Resources for Chapter 19

Here you will find resources mentioned in Chapter 19, supplemental resources, videos, as well as new and updated resources.

ShakeupLearningBook.com/19

Discussion Questions

- What did you like about this planning process?
- What would you change?

Chapter 19 Actions

- Think about what you have planned so far, and revisit the resources from the previous chapters to think through your ideas. Make revisions as needed.
- Share your Dynamic Learning Experience with a colleague, a teacher friend, another educator, or on social media or the Shake Up Learning community before you implement and ask for honest feedback.

Chapter 20
Go for It!

If you wait for perfect conditions,
you will never get anything done.
—Ecclesiastes 11:4

Implementation

Ready to test out your learning experience? It's time to implement. You've done the work; you've carefully and purposefully planned; now let's jump in and try it! Are you uncomfortable yet? I want to make you uncomfortable! Remember the chapter about the importance of risk-taking? It's time to go all-in!

Review the practical tips for planning and facilitation to give yourself every tool on the teacher utility belt. You've got this! Stay positive. Whether this is brand new for you or a new twist on things you've already been doing, take things to the next level. Push yourself and your students to new heights. No matter your experience level, everyone can use this framework to kick things up a notch. If things don't go as planned, that's okay. There's a first try for everything. A first attempt in learning.

Got questions? Concerned about trying something new? Let's chat! Share your fears, questions, and concerns in the Shake Up Learning community (shakeup.link/community) or on Twitter with the hashtag #ShakeUpLearning.

Honest Reflection

How did it go? Reflection is an important piece of the learning process, and it's time to be honest with yourself about what went well, what didn't, and what you would change. Being a teacher is a tough job. It seems we are always in a hurry. Do you reflect or leave yourself notes about your lesson plans? You should. There were many times I would forget and then deliver the learning experience the next year, only to repeat past mistakes or forget to make minor tweaks and changes that could have made it more successful.

I want you to reflect on everything—the planning, the implementation, and everything in between. Your reflection can take any form you choose. Go old school and journal it with pen and paper. Open up Google Docs and reflect digitally. Have a blog? Share it on your blog. Like to sketch your notes? Sketch out your reflection with paper, pens, markers, and stickers, or go digital with your favorite sketching app. If you like talking it out, record a video confessional a la *The Real World*, the groundbreaking MTV reality show that would have participants go into a private room, face the camera, and spill their guts. This strategy has been used in countless other reality shows since then. Of course, if you don't want to go all *Keeping up with the Kardashians* or *The Real Housewives of Beverly Hills*, just use the camera on your device to share your reflection in a simple video.

Answer the following questions in your reflection:

- What went well? (Start off with the positive.)
- What didn't go well?
- What would you change?
- Was it dynamic?
- How was it different from other learning experiences you have facilitated in the past?

Feel free to add any other comments, suggestions for other teachers, or fun anecdotes.

Reflection Strategies and Tools

- Write about it.
- Blog about it.
- Sketch it.
- Make a video confessional with YouTube, Flipgrid, or other tool of your choice.

Revise and Share Your DLE

Depending on what you learned during your implementation, it can be helpful to revise your DLE before you share it. There are almost always at least a few little tweaks that can improve it for next time or for the next teacher. After all, you want to offer other educators the best version of your learning experience. Be sure to add comments and recommendations that might be useful for other teachers who may want to use your Dynamic Learning Experience in their classrooms.

Next step? Share it with the world! Remember what I said about going all in, taking a risk, and the importance of sharing. I want this database full of ideas for teachers of all walks, a teacher just like YOU! Perfection is the enemy of done. Please share it! Of course, you can share your DLE in multiple ways, but I would like you to contribute to my Dynamic Learning Experience database (shakeup.link/DLdatabase) so other teachers can find your experience and learn from you. To share your DLE, use the form at shakeup.link/DLEform. Feel free to share it on social media and in the Shake Up Learning community.

Online Resources for Chapter 20

Here you will find resources mentioned in Chapter 20, supplemental resources, videos, as well as new and updated resources.

ShakeUpLearningBook.com/20

Chapter 20 Actions

- Write, blog, video, or sketch a reflection about the implementation of your Dynamic Learning Experience:
    - What went well? (Start off with the positive.)
    - What didn't go well?
    - What would you change?
    - Was it dynamic?
    - How was it different from other learning experiences you have facilitated in the past?
    - Feel free to add any other comments, suggestions for other teachers, or fun anecdotes.
    - Share and discuss your experience with a colleague to help you debrief.
- Make any necessary revisions to your template so you can make it even better next time.
- Add the reflection to your template and submit to the DL database: shakeup.link/DLdatabase.

How Will You Shake Up Learning?

Don't be afraid to go against the grain, try an out-of-the-box approach, or look a little crazy to your colleagues. We all learned to teach in a certain way, but that doesn't mean there aren't new and better ways to reach our learners. Don't assume everyone has heard the message. There are so many educators who simply don't get it, who haven't heard the news. Think of yourself like a learning evangelist. Each voice has the power to reach someone new.

Traditional learning with desks in rows and a teacher in the front of the room serving as the keeper of all knowledge simply doesn't work anymore. Rethink your assignments. Be an uncommon educator! Don't follow the crowd. Let the crowd follow you. Ignite the ordinary. Stop waiting for the paradigm shift to happen. Dare to believe the impossible. Teach with audaciousness. Be bold. Have audacious faith in students. You are a professional, and you know what's best for the learners in your classroom. Let that be your guide as you step out of the old ways of teaching and develop new and somewhat disruptive methods of developing future-ready students.

You. You have the power to make a difference in the lives of hundreds of children and the future of education as we know it. You. You have the power to cultivate passions, new ideas, and new perspectives. You. You have the power to Shake Up Learning!

One Last Reminder...

We've covered a wealth of information in this book, but that doesn't mean your learning should end here. In fact, I've created a companion website that includes many resources mentioned throughout this book.

Here are just a few things I've included:

- The *Shake Up Learning* Quick-Start Guide, which is a printable reference guide of the main ideas, strategies, and tips from the book
- A dedicated webpage for each chapter of the book, including clickable resources
- The Dynamic Learning Experience searchable database of lessons from teachers like you where you can find ideas AND share your own

> Ignite the ordinary. Stop waiting for the paradigm shift to happen. Dare to believe the impossible. Teach with audaciousness. Be bold. Have audacious faith in students.

- Information about the companion course, The Dynamic Learning Workshop, a self-paced online course to enrich your learning with the book even more
- Special bonus materials and downloads

I will be adding more goodies to this website in the months to come. So if you're interested in expanding on what you've learned in this book, check out the following link:

ShakeupLearningBook.com

The Companion Course: The Dynamic Learning Workshop

In addition to the community and website of free resources to support you, I am also offering an online course: The Dynamic Learning Workshop. This is a workshop designed to go deeper than just a book study and to not only explore the ideas in the book but to bring it to life through video-based learning and support.

To find out more about the Dynamic Learning Workshop and how to enroll, go to **shakeup.link/DLworkshop.**

- Bulk pricing available for large groups, campuses, or entire school districts.
- Purchase orders accepted

Thank You

Finally, to you, the reader: Thank you for allowing *Shake Up Learning* to be a part of your teaching life. Let's keep connecting on social media and the Shake Up Learning Community. Please let me know how you are doing, and if there is ever anything I can do to help you, please don't hesitate to ask.

Okay, y'all. Now stop reading and start creating!

Credits and Acknowledgments

The Shake Up Learning avatar was created by my talented nephew, Keaton Raney.

Thank you to Amber Teamann, Melinda Miller, and Tom Spall for allowing me to share your fantastic work.

Special thanks to those who contributed learning experience examples:

- Christine Pinto
- Carrie Baughcum
- Matt Hawkins and Jeremy Badiner
- Sylvia Duckworth
- Sean Fahey
- Karly Moura
- Michele Waggoner
- Heather Marshall
- Becky Ogbouma

You are some of the hardest working teachers I know! Thank you for all you do and share with the educational world!

Bring the Power of Kasey Bell and the *Shake Up Learning* Message to Your School, District, or Event!

With more than ten years' experience as a speaker, presenter, and professional learning facilitator, and fifteen years' experience as an educator, Kasey brings her unique brand of practical teaching ideas, inspiration, bold personality, and southern charm to every engagement. She has traveled the world delivering inspirational keynotes, workshops, and interactive conference presentations at world-renown conferences, school districts, private schools, and even hosting her own events. Kasey has spoken at the International Society for Technology in Education (ISTE) Conference, Texas Computer Educators Association (TCEA) Convention, the Teach Tech Play Conference in Melbourne, Australia, iPadpalooza, Google Summits, and is regularly invited by Google to present to educators around the globe.

What Teachers Are Saying about Kasey Bell . . .

"Kasey Bell was amazing. I appreciated her energy, expertise, and experience. The examples, strategies, and resources she shared were so valuable and accessible for people at all levels. Thank you so much for the opportunity to hear her speak and learn from/with her. I could spend hours hearing her talk about her ideas."

— ERLC Innovation Summit in Edmonton, Canada, participant

"You are AMAZING! I am inspired every time I hear you present! My brain is in overload! Can't wait to try the new things I learned today in Google Keep! Thank you!!"

—Tonya Gaunt

"Thank you for inspiring me further to release control and put the power of learning into the hands of my students. Whenever I allow them to use their creativity, they never cease to amaze me. Thank you!!!!!"

—Christi Corbin

"Awesome information, takeaways that can be used in the classroom tomorrow. Thanks for sharing your resources. You were very engaging and motivational."

—Dara Kappel

"Thank you for providing information in a way that makes sense! I usually go to tech-based PD and feel lost, but you were amazing at making Google Classroom feel easy to use and accessible!

I now feel like implementing Google Classroom for this school year is the right decision—be prepared for emails asking questions as I get the hang of it!☺"

—Anastasia Armstreet

"As always, Kasey delivers amazing resources in informative and concise presentations. Thank you so much for your thoughtful organization of all things Google."

—Lesley Garcia

"Best session I went to at FETC . . . So much wonderful information and every bit of it useful!"

—Luanne Rowland

"Your passion in what you do is inspiring. I left your class with a lot of great information that I will pass to my fellow teachers. Thank you."

—Joseph Tellez

"If you are attending a conference, follow these steps:
1. Search by presenter.
2. Find Kasey Bell.
3. Put all her sessions on your schedule!
You will learn so much and have a great time doing it!"

—Stacy Menifee

Popular Presentation Topics Include

- Be Dynamic and Shake Up Learning (keynote)
- The Dynamic Learning Workshop (in person and online)
- Digital Differentiation with G Suite
- Teach Like the Tonight Show
- Shake Up Learning with G Suite
- Geeking Out Over Google Classroom

For more information, go to shakeup.link/workwithme

The Dynamic Learning Workshop: shakeup.link/DLWorkshop

- Online or in person
- Bulk discounts for ten or more participants

Connect with Kasey

✉ Kasey@ShakeUpLearning.com

🐦 @ShakeUpLearning

🌐 ShakeUpLearning.com

More From

Teach Like a PIRATE

Increase Student Engagement, Boost Your Creativity, and Transform Your Life as an Educator

By Dave Burgess (@BurgessDave)

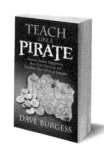

New York Times' bestseller *Teach Like a PIRATE* sparked a worldwide educational revolution with its passionate teaching manifesto and dynamic student-engagement strategies. Translated into multiple languages, it sparks outrageously creative lessons and life-changing student experiences.

P is for PIRATE

Inspirational ABCs for Educators

By Dave and Shelley Burgess (@Burgess_Shelley)

In *P is for Pirate*, husband-and-wife team Dave and Shelley Burgess tap personal experiences of seventy educators to inspire others to create fun and exciting places to learn. It's a wealth of imaginative and creative ideas that makes learning and teaching more fulfilling than ever before.

The Innovator's Mindset

Empower Learning, Unleash Talent, and Lead a Culture of Creativity

By George Couros (@gcouros)

In *The Innovator's Mindset*, teachers and administrators discover that compliance to a scheduled curriculum hinders student innovation, critical thinking, and creativity. To become forward-thinking leaders, students must be empowered to wonder and explore.

Pure Genius

Building a Culture of Innovation and Taking 20% Time to the Next Level

By Don Wettrick (@DonWettrick)

Collaboration—with experts, students, and other educators—helps create interesting and even life-changing opportunities for learning. In *Pure Genius*, Don Wettrick inspires and equips educators with a systematic blueprint for beating classroom boredom and teaching innovation.

Learn Like a PIRATE
Empower Your Students to Collaborate, Lead, and Succeed
By Paul Solarz (@PaulSolarz)

Passing grades don't equip students for life and career responsibilities. *Learn Like a PIRATE* shows how risk-taking and exploring passions in stimulating, motivating, supportive, self-directed classrooms creates students capable of making smart, responsible decisions on their own.

Ditch That Textbook
Free Your Teaching and Revolutionize Your Classroom
By Matt Miller (@jmattmiller)

Ditch That Textbook creates a support system, toolbox, and manifesto that can free teachers from outdated textbooks. Miller empowers them to untether themselves, throw out meaningless, pedestrian teaching and learning practices, and evolve and revolutionize their classrooms.

50 Things You Can Do with Google Classroom
By Alice Keeler and Libbi Miller (@alicekeeler, @MillerLibbi)

50 Things You Can Do with Google Classroom provides a thorough overview of this GAfE app and shortens the teacher learning curve for introducing technology in the classroom. Keeler and Miller's ideas, instruction, and screenshots help teachers go digital with this powerful tool.

50 Things to Go Further with Google Classroom
A Student-Centered Approach
By Alice Keeler and Libbi Miller (@alicekeeler, @MillerLibbi)

In *50 Things to Go Further with Google Classroom: A Student-Centered Approach*, authors and educators Alice Keeler and Libbi Miller help teachers create a digitally rich, engaging, student-centered environment that taps the power of individualized learning using Google Classroom.

140 Twitter Tips for Educators

Get Connected, Grow Your Professional Learning Network, and Reinvigorate Your Career

By Brad Currie, Billy Krakower, and Scott Rocco (@bradmcurrie, @wkrakower, @ScottRRocco)

In *140 Twitter Tips for Educators*, #Satchat hosts and founders of Evolving Educators, Brad Currie, Billy Krakower, and Scott Rocco, offer step-by-step instruction on Twitter basics and building an online following within Twitter's vibrant network of educational professionals.

Master the Media

How Teaching Media Literacy Can Save Our Plugged-In World

By Julie Smith (@julnilsmith)

Master the Media explains media history, purpose, and messaging so teachers and parents can empower students with critical-thinking skills which lead to informed choices, the ability to differentiate between truth and lies, and discern perception from reality. Media literacy can save the world.

The Zen Teacher

Creating Focus, Simplicity, and Tranquility in the Classroom

By Dan Tricarico (@thezenteacher)

Unrushed and fully focused, teachers influence—even improve—the future when they maximize performance and improve their quality of life. In *The Zen Teacher*, Dan Tricarico offers practical, easy-to-use techniques to develop a non-religious Zen practice and thrive in the classroom.

eXPlore Like a Pirate

Gamification and Game-Inspired Course Design to Engage, Enrich, and Elevate Your Learners

By Michael Matera (@MrMatera)

Create an experiential, collaborative, and creative world with classroom game designer and educator Michael Matera's game-based learning book, *eXPlore Like a Pirate*. Matera helps teachers apply motivational gameplay techniques and enhance curriculum with gamification strategies.

Your School Rocks . . . So Tell People!
Passionately Pitch and Promote the Positives Happening on Your Campus
By Ryan McLane and Eric Lowe (@McLane_Ryan, @EricLowe21)

Your School Rocks . . . So Tell People! helps schools create effective social media communication strategies that keep students' families and the community connected to what's going on at school, offering more than seventy immediately actionable tips with easy-to-follow instructions and video tutorial links.

Play Like a Pirate
Engage Students with Toys, Games, and Comics
By Quinn Rollins (@jedikermit)

In *Play Like a Pirate*, Quinn Rollins offers practical, engaging strategies and resources that make it easy to integrate fun into your curriculum. Regardless of grade level, serious learning can be seriously fun with inspirational ideas that engage students in unforgettable ways.

The Classroom Chef
Sharpen Your Lessons. Season Your Classes. Make Math Meaningful.
By John Stevens and Matt Vaudrey (@Jstevens009, @MrVaudrey)

With imagination and preparation, every teacher can be *The Classroom Chef* using John Stevens and Matt Vaudrey's secret recipes, ingredients, and tips that help students "get" math. Use ideas as-is, or tweak to create enticing educational meals that engage students.

How Much Water Do We Have?
5 Success Principles for Conquering Any Challenge and Thriving in Times of Change
By Pete Nunweiler with Kris Nunweiler

Stressed out, overwhelmed, or uncertain at work or home? It could be figurative dehydration.

How Much Water Do We Have? identifies five key elements necessary for success of any goal, life transition, or challenge. Learn to find, acquire, and use the 5 Waters of Success.

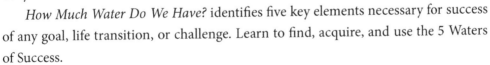

The Writing on the Classroom Wall
How Posting Your Most Passionate Beliefs about Education Can Empower Your Students, Propel Your Growth, and Lead to a Lifetime of Learning
By Steve Wyborney (@SteveWyborney)

Big ideas lead to deeper learning, but they don't have to be profound to have profound impact. Teacher Steve Wyborney explains why and how sharing ideas sharpens and refines them. It's okay if some ideas fall off the wall; what matters most is sharing and discussing.

Kids Deserve It!
Pushing Boundaries and Challenging Conventional Thinking
By Todd Nesloney and Adam Welcome (@TechNinjaTodd, @awelcome)

Think big. Make learning fun and meaningful. In *Kids Deserve It!* Nesloney and Welcome offer high-tech, high-touch, and highly engaging practices that inspire risk-taking and shake up the status quo on behalf of your students. Rediscover why you became an educator, too!

LAUNCH
Using Design Thinking to Boost Creativity and Bring Out the Maker in Every Student
By John Spencer and A.J. Juliani (@spencerideas, @ajjuliani)

When students identify themselves as makers, inventors, and creators, they discover powerful problem-solving and critical-thinking skills. Their imaginations and creativity will shape our future. John Spencer and A.J. Juliani's *LAUNCH* process dares you to innovate and empower them.

Instant Relevance
Using Today's Experiences to Teach Tomorrow's Lessons
By Denis Sheeran (@MathDenisNJ)

Learning sticks when it's relevant to students. In *Instant Relevance*, author and keynote speaker Denis Sheeran equips you to create engaging lessons from experiences and events that matter to students while helping them make meaningful connections between the real world and the classroom.

Escaping the School Leader's Dunk Tank
How to Prevail When Others Want to See You Drown
By Rebecca Coda and Rick Jetter (@RebeccaCoda, @RickJetter)

Dunk-tank situations—discrimination, bad politics, revenge, or ego-driven coworkers—can make an educator's life miserable. Coda and Jetter (dunk-tank survivors themselves) share real-life stories and insightful research to equip school leaders with tools to survive and, better yet, avoid getting "dunked."

Start. Right. Now.
Teach and Lead for Excellence
By Todd Whitaker, Jeff Zoul, and Jimmy Casas (@ToddWhitaker, @Jeff_Zoul, @casas_jimmy)

Excellent leaders and teachers *Know the Way, Show the Way, Go the Way, and Grow Each Day*. Whitaker, Zoul, and Casas share four key behaviors of excellence from educators across the U.S. and motivate to put you on the right path.

Lead Like a PIRATE
Make School Amazing for Your Students and Staff
By Shelley Burgess and Beth Houf (@Burgess_Shelley, @BethHouf)

Lead Like a PIRATE maps out character traits necessary to captain a school or district. You'll learn where to find treasure already in your classrooms and schools—and bring out the best in educators. Find encouragement in your relentless quest to make school amazing for everyone!

Teaching Math with Google Apps
50 G Suite Activities
By Alice Keeler and Diana Herrington (@AliceKeeler, @mathdiana)

Teaching Math with Google Apps meshes the easy student/teacher interaction of Google Apps with G Suite that empowers student creativity and critical thinking. Keeler and Herrington demonstrate fifty ways to bring math classes into the twenty-first century with easy-to-use technology.

Table Talk Math
A Practical Guide for Bringing Math into Everyday Conversations
By John Stevens (@Jstevens009)

In *Table Talk Math*, John Stevens offers parents—and teachers—ideas for initiating authentic, math-based, everyday conversations that get kids to notice and pique their curiosity about the numbers, patterns, and equations in the world around them.

Shift This!
How to Implement Gradual Change for Massive Impact in Your Classroom
By Joy Kirr (@JoyKirr)

Establishing a student-led culture focused on individual responsibility and personalized learning *is* possible, sustainable, and even easy when it happens little by little. In *Shift This!*, Joy Kirr details gradual shifts in thinking, teaching, and approach for massive impact in your classroom.

Unmapped Potential
An Educator's Guide to Lasting Change
By Julie Hasson and Missy Lennard (@PPrincipals)

Overwhelmed and overworked? You're not alone, but it can get better. You simply need the right map to guide you from frustrated to fulfilled. *Unmapped Potential* offers advice and practical strategies to forge a unique path to becoming the educator and person you want to be.

Shattering the Perfect Teacher Myth
6 Truths That Will Help You THRIVE as an Educator
By Aaron Hogan (@aaron_hogan)

Author and educator Aaron Hogan helps shatter the idyllic "perfect teacher" myth, which erodes self-confidence with unrealistic expectations and sets teachers up for failure. His book equips educators with strategies that help them shift out of survival mode and THRIVE.

Social LEADia

Moving Students from Digital Citizenship to Digital Leadership

By Jennifer Casa-Todd (@JCasaTodd)

A networked society requires students to leverage social media to connect to people, passions, and opportunities to grow and make a difference. Social *LEADia* helps shift focus at school and home from digital citizenship to digital leadership and equip students for the future.

Spark Learning

3 Keys to Embracing the Power of Student Curiosity

By Ramsey Musallam (@ramusallam)

Inspired by his popular TED Talk "3 Rules to Spark Learning," Musallam combines brain science research, proven teaching methods, and his personal story to empower you to improve your students' learning experiences by inspiring inquiry and harnessing its benefits.

Ditch That Homework

Practical Strategies to Help Make Homework Obsolete

By Matt Miller and Alice Keeler (@jmattmiller, @alicekeeler)

In *Ditch That Homework*, Miller and Keeler discuss the pros and cons of homework, why it's assigned, and what life could look like without it. They evaluate research, share parent and teacher insights, then make a convincing case for ditching it for effective and personalized learning methods.

The Four O'Clock Faculty

A Rogue Guide to Revolutionizing Professional Development

By Rich Czyz (@RACzyz)

In *The Four O'Clock Faculty*, Rich identifies ways to make professional learning meaningful, efficient, and, above all, personally relevant. It's a practical guide to revolutionize PD, revealing why some is so awful and what you can do to change the model for the betterment of everyone.

ᴊrize

.ry Student. Every Day. Whatever It Takes.

By Jimmy Casas (@casas_jimmy)

Culturize dives into what it takes to cultivate a community of learners who embody innately human traits our world desperately needs—kindness, honesty, and compassion. Casas's stories reveal how "soft skills" can be honed while exceeding academic standards of twenty-first-century learning.

Code Breaker

Increase Creativity, Remix Assessment, and Develop a Class of Coder Ninjas!

By Brian Aspinall (@mraspinall)

You don't have to be a "computer geek" to use coding to turn curriculum expectations into student skills. Use *Code Breaker* to teach students how to identify problems, develop solutions, and use computational thinking to apply and demonstrate learning.

The Wild Card

7 Steps to an Educator's Creative Breakthrough

By Hope and Wade King (@hopekingteach, @wadeking7)

The Kings facilitate a creative breakthrough in the classroom with *The Wild Card*, a step-by-step guide to drawing on your authentic self to deliver your content creatively and be the wild card who changes the game for your learners.

Stories from Webb

The Ideas, Passions, and Convictions of a Principal and His School Family

By Todd Nesloney (@TechNinjaTodd)

Stories from Webb goes right to the heart of education. Told by award-winning principal Todd Nesloney and his dedicated team of staff and teachers, this book reminds you why you became an educator. Relatable stories reinvigorate and may inspire you to tell your own!

The Principled Principal

10 Principles for Leading Exceptional Schools

By Jeffrey Zoul and Anthony McConnell (@Jeff_Zou, @mcconnellaw)

Zoul and McConnell know from personal experience that the role of school principal is one of the most challenging and the most rewarding in education. Using relatable stories and real-life examples, they reveal ten core values that will empower you to work and lead with excellence.

The Limitless School

Creative Ways to Solve the Culture Puzzle

By Abe Hege and Adam Dovico (@abehege, @adamdovico)

Being intentional about creating a positive culture is imperative for your school's success. This book identifies the nine pillars that support a positive school culture and explains how each stakeholder has a vital role to play in the work of making schools safe, inviting, and dynamic.

Google Apps for Littles

Believe They Can

By Christine Pinto and Alice Keeler (@PintoBeanz11, @alicekeeler)

Learn how to tap into students' natural curiosity using technology. Pinto and Keeler share a wealth of innovative ways to integrate digital tools in the primary classroom to make learning engaging and relevant for even the youngest of today's twenty-first-century learners.

About the Author

Kasey Bell is part sparkling smile, part witty personality, and a whole heap of passion as big as Texas—go big or go home, y'all! As a former middle school teacher with nearly fifteen years in education, Kasey has made it her mission to be a disruptor of the boring and to push the bounds of traditional teaching and learning.

Kasey found her true passion in digital learning, and with a master's degree in educational technology and a whole bunch of crazy ideas, she migrated to the role of instructional technologist for Leander ISD. Now, Kasey is a Digital Learning Consultant for Region 10 Education Service Center in Richardson, Texas. As her passion grew, so did her need to share and connect, and Kasey started sharing her passions through her blog, ShakeUpLearning.com.

Kasey is an engaging, innovative, from-the-heart sharer who inspires educators while transforming their teaching with original, dynamic, and use-tomorrow ideas for student choice, differentiation, and technology integration. Whether it is learning from home through online courses, conference workshops, or as a keynote speaker, Kasey is a relentless innovator of ideas and a devoted transformer of classrooms and teaching.

Through teacher-empowering publications and award-winning educational resources at ShakeUpLearning.com, learner-driven workshops and presentations, and co-hosting The Google Teacher Tribe weekly podcast, Kasey proves why we should never settle for the static and boring when it comes to bringing out the very best in our students, and we should always strive to *Shake Up Learning!*